THE
NEW
MODERN
HOUSE

REDEFINING
FUNCTIONALISM

LAURENCE KING

First published in Great Britain in 2010
This paperback edition first published in 2012
by Laurence King Publishing Ltd
361–373 City Road
London EC1V 1LR
United Kingdom
Tel: + 44 20 7841 6900
Fax: + 44 20 7841 6910
e-mail: enquiries@laurenceking.com
www.laurenceking.com

This book was produced by Laurence King
Publishing Ltd, London

Design by Sarah Douglas and Lee Belcher
Picture Research by Anna Stathaki

Front cover photo: ©Ludger Paffrath
Back cover photo: ©Nina Baisch, Dipl.-Des.
(FH) M.A., Konstanz, Germany

ISBN: 978 1 78067 025 6

Printed in China

THE NEW MODERN HOUSE

REDEFINING FUNCTIONALISM

Jonathan Bell & Ellie Stathaki

Laurence King Publishing

CONTENTS

Introduction

Rural

Suburban

Urban

INTRODUCTION

The house is not a machine. Instead, it is a collection of systems, structures, aspirations and memories...

In any debate about modernity, the residential design ideal and the form of the contemporary house, it seems that utility, aspiration and intention are often overlooked. The contemporary house has become defined by a combination of elaborate formal invention and the rigorous and relentless application of styles and materials that have come to symbolize the genre.

This book is about a new functionalism in domestic architecture. The projects illustrated within are purposeful and pragmatic, always modern, yet not hidebound by stylistic conventions or aesthetic preconceptions. Functionalism is at the heart of architecture – all architecture – a universal quality that has been co-opted by various movements and factions over the centuries.

The fundamental need for a structure to be useful, practical and fit for purpose was inherent in the very first human buildings. The Roman scholar and architect Vitruvius wrote in *De Architectura* (usually dated to around 25BC) that a building must embody the qualities of *firmitas, utilitas, venustas*, or 'firmness, commodity and delight'. Firmness and delight refer to quality and aesthetics respectively, but ultimately it is the 'commodity' that concerns us most; then, as now, a building must fulfil its purpose (from the original meaning of the word as being something that offers convenience or advantage).

The Vitruvian ideal continues to underpin the role of the architect, binding together aesthetics and function, while simultaneously elevating the image of both architect and architecture to a central position in society. But as we enter the current era, we find that the notion of 'commodity' has been thoroughly debased, with the result that the 'advantage' in architecture is often derived not from use or function, but from the perceived sophistication, intelligence and ability of the designer and the photogenic attributes of the design. Modern architecture has become increasingly concerned with the iconic rather than the convenient.

Once it became apparent that the function of display and communication could be of equal importance to the activity within a building, 'functionalism' fell out of favour. With this realization came a rift, a theoretical fissure that was adapted and claimed by the conflicting voices in the architectural scene. Contemporary architecture has emerged as perpetually dualistic. Ethics and aesthetics. Modern and traditional. Minimal and maximal. Deconstructed and constructivist. The slow, steady, evolutionary development of modern architecture was effectively derailed and opened up into multiple pathways, criss-crossing, splitting and branching off, blurring the original principles of an architecture committed to social progress through technological innovation.

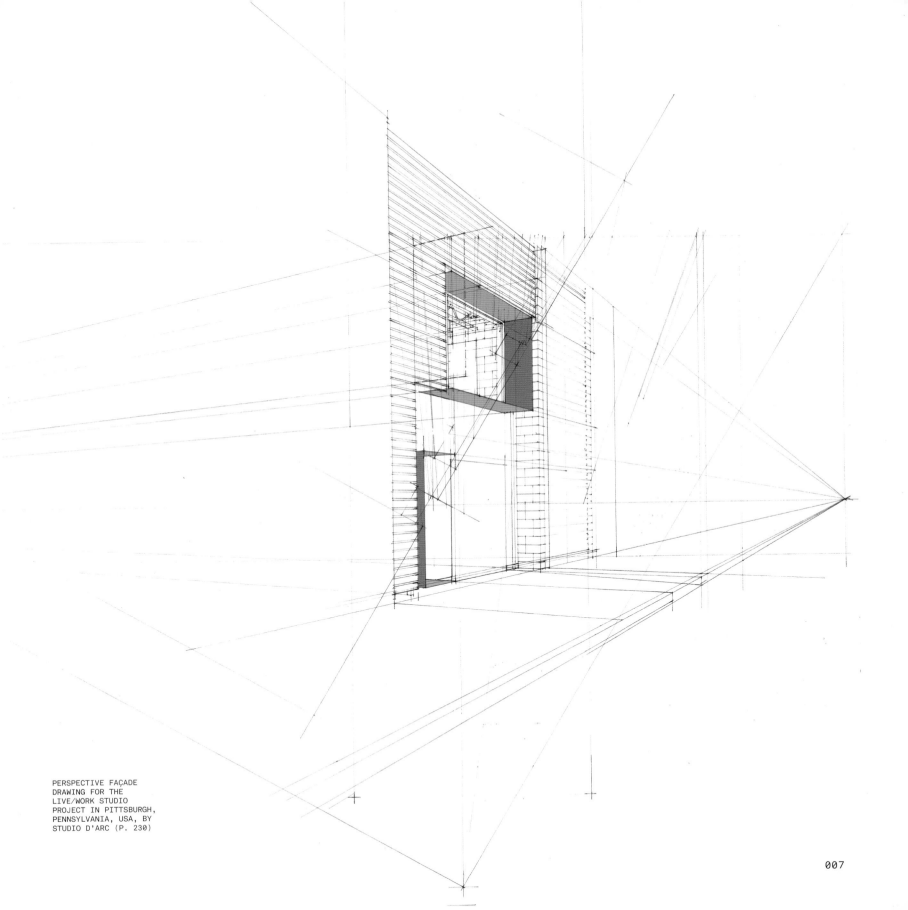

PERSPECTIVE FAÇADE
DRAWING FOR THE
LIVE/WORK STUDIO
PROJECT IN PITTSBURGH,
PENNSYLVANIA, USA, BY
STUDIO D'ARC (P. 230)

01
LE CORBUSIER'S MAISONS
JAOUL, IN A SUBURB OF
PARIS, FRANCE (1951)

02
BRADLEY HOUSE AT MADISON,
WISCONSIN, USA, BY LOUIS
SULLIVAN (1910)

03
THE UPPER LAWN PAVILION
(ALSO KNOWN AS THE SOLAR
PAVILION), WILTSHIRE, UK,
BY ALISON AND PETER
SMITHSON (1962)

01

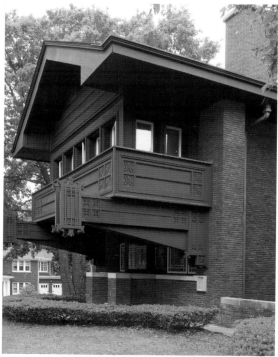

02

03

Both the Modernists, with their machined perfectionism, and the Arts and Crafts movement, with its craft-infused deliberations, defined their work through its functional value. Design reformers such as William Morris believed that visual excess was morally unwholesome, all the more so if it was bereft of human involvement in its creation. Louis Sullivan's phrase 'form ever follows function, and this is the law'[1] was enthusiastically adopted by architects of every creed. The British architect W.R. Lethaby wrote in 1936, 'we have to prune our building forms as we prune a fruit tree and sternly cut away dead wood. Whenever we concentrate on some directing datum, some reality like health, serviceableness or even perfect cheapness, true style will certainly arise as the expression of this and the other human qualities embodied.'[2]

The 'New Functionalism' described in this book is a constant thread of background static, running beneath the noise of architectural discourse. It is a sensibility, not a movement; an approach and a mindset, rather than a manifesto. The modern iteration of this sensibility is demonstrated in these 50 contemporary projects from around the world. Unified by their concern for the everyday, from patterns of domesticity to a quiet reverence for simplicity, these houses demonstrate a common approach without sharing a distinct aesthetic.

The historical precedents for New Functionalism are many and varied. Respect for vernacular forms, spirit of place and historical context are rarely absent, yet there is also a strong sense of technical innovation and aesthetic experimentation, and a willingness to re-appraise and develop past approaches. One of the key architectural movements concerned with the value of the quotidian and with its role in anchoring architecture to human needs and sensibilities was New Brutalism. This casually damning name was given to a small group of progressive post-war British architects, led – in a loose sense – by Alison and Peter Smithson. The work was chronicled and labelled 'the New Brutalism' in a book of the same name by Reyner Banham in 1966, a shorthand that originally had an aesthetic rather than an intellectual focus – it was a smart way of lumping together the emerging rough-sided, asymmetrical buildings, with their bunker-like façades and austere, heavy-handed detailing.

'New Brutalism' swiftly became pejorative, as the physical and psychological connections being identified between concrete, bunkers, aggression and alienation seeped from the pages of the architectural press into the comment pages; social function and aesthetic style were conflated. The New Brutalists found themselves playing an integral – if largely unwarranted – role in the evolution of the post-war Modernist architectural aesthetic, forever linked to its more unsuccessful moments. Today, Brutalism continues to be associated with 'carbuncles', conjuring up substandard, pitilessly drab accommodation and the unyielding and blinkered paternalism of the autocratic architect.

With hindsight, Banham's self-confessed failure to convey the thought processes behind the aesthetic are understandable. The Brutalists' concrete architecture had such a strong physical presence that any symbolic messages were almost inevitably muddled. On the one hand, it spoke of dominance, power and aggression, demonstrated by the remarkably avant-garde forms of the Second World War beach-head defences along the northern French coastline.[3] On the other, the buildings themselves conveyed a sense of honest manual labour, through their rough concrete surface, permanently marked with the imprint of the wooden shuttering used to form it.

The first exponents of Brutalism were not slavishly imitating the wartime bunker, with all its unhappy associations. Instead, they believed they were stripping back the Modernist aesthetic to reveal honesty and integrity, rather than purity and simplicity (by which point the latter had descended into yet another form of stylistic overlay). At the forefront of the movement, although never its leader in the conventional way, was Le Corbusier, whose use of raw concrete – *beton brut* – gave Brutalism its name and its defining characteristics.

Le Corbusier's Maisons Jaoul project was one of the prototypes of the New Brutalist movement, a composition of two private houses built just outside Paris in the mid-1950s. The combination of brick infill with exposed concrete frame gave these houses a – for the time – unique appearance of toughness, concerned not with definitions of quality relating to finish, richness of materials or meticulous craftsmanship, but with an atmosphere that was hitherto considered impossible – or undesirable – to replicate. The rough textures of the houses appeared hand-finished, not a product of the machine – this ran contrary to Le Corbusier's role as the harbinger of the machine age. Some 30 years after the euphoric techno-rhetoric of *Vers Une Architecture*, the Jaoul houses represented a matured sensibility, not a call to pure, unsentimental reason.

Architectural history is not a linear process, but Corbusier's Jaoul houses marked a point from which several branches of thought can be seen to sprout. For example, the Brazilian Paulista School that began in the 1950s stressed heavy structure, naked concrete finishes and a more primal, elemental architectural massing. Named for a group of architects working out of São Paulo (including Joaquim Guedes and Paulo Mendes da Rocha), the Paulista approach had clear Corbusian influences. In Japan, the Metabolist school favoured raw functionalism on a hitherto unprecedented scale, eschewing formal and traditional architectural approaches in favour of a fresh start, a megastructural future. In Europe, a far more sympathetic form of contemporary architecture rose up in the form of Critical Regionalism, a reaction against Modernism's tendency towards universal forms, reintroducing context and vernacular. In Australia, the work of Glenn Murcutt illustrates a similar functional yet site-specific sensibility, combining integration with nature, sustainable building systems and local construction techniques to create a series of highly refined, yet ultra functional, houses.

In Britain and many other European countries, Brutalism found itself pressed into social service in the form of large-scale housing and arts projects, heroic yet also fundamentally ordinary and down-to-earth. This was architecture shaped by prevailing progressive ideology. Unfortunately, idealism was overwhelmed by a fascination with aesthetics: what had been considered down-to-earth, honest and truthful was decried as alienating, inhuman and élitist. '[The New Brutalism's] chief propagandist, Reyner Banham, pondered whether the idiom was an "ethic" or an "aesthetic", so firmly marked was it by social concerns. He claimed that its architects were the equivalents of the "angry young men" of the '50s – they were of "red-brick extraction", products of post-war class mobility, usually northerners.'[4]

The schism between intention and interpretation blighted the Brutalist movement from the outset. The Smithsons also lamented how the emphasis on aesthetics subsumed their attempts to negotiate new architectural conditions and technologies in a democratic, economical fashion. In Banham's original book, they were at pains to point out that 'any discussion of Brutalism will miss the point if it does not take into account Brutalism's attempt to be objective about "reality", the cultural objectives of society, its urges, its techniques and so on. Brutalism tries to face up to a mass-production society, and drag a rough poetry out of the confused and powerful forces that are at work.' Up to now Brutalism has largely been discussed in stylistic terms, where in essence it is ethical.

In their 2001 book *As Found*, Claude Lichtenstein and Thomas Schregenberger created a cultural history of the era of ferment that generated the Smithsons' theoretical and aesthetic stance, shared by like-minded compatriots in art, design, photography, journalism and theatre. *As Found*, they wrote, 'is the tendency to engage with what is there, to recognize the existing, to follow its traces with interest'.[5] The New Functional aesthetic takes this modest dictum to heart. The editors continue that 'ultimately, the term means taking note of things in a radical way'. Domestic architecture is the realm of things, a constructed space specific to individual lives.

In this respect, the pragmatic approach chronicled in *As Found* can be seen as a response to the intractability of the world, countering stubborn resistance to change with an equally stubborn, almost perverse, desire to seek out beauty, or a new definition of beauty, within everything. Within architecture, this is a radical position to take. The idea of perfection was – and still is – held as the central obsession of the Modern movement, which makes the 'machine for living' the only possible solution for any particular problem.

The inevitable anti-aesthetic of the New Brutalists was diametrically opposed to the carefully staged and structured vignettes of the Modernist approach, and by implication, the way in which contemporary architecture was presented to the world through heroic, almost abstract, photographic imagery. A functionalist house, therefore, cannot be reduced down to a single, artfully composed photograph: it is the representation of a constant, ongoing life.

By not aiming for a glossy, well-finished perfection, the New Brutalist movement marked the start of a schism within the British strain of post-war modern architecture. The architect Patrick Lynch has talked about the British high-tech movement as essentially a continuation of the engineering prowess of the Victorian era, with all the connotations of superhuman ability, strength and dominance over the natural order.[6] At the same time, another strand of British architecture, represented by the Smithsons and James Stirling, Trevor Dannatt, Colin St John Wilson and others, was intent on creating a more humane, Aalto-esque strand of architectural design that determined flexibility to be an innately human quality, not a mechanical factor. Their architecture was anti-aesthetic in the sense of abhorring the grand gesture and the tyranny of symmetry. According to Lynch, this approach ultimately died out, killed off from lack of establishment support, by Stirling's early death and by the stylistic and economic dominance of both conventional high-tech – one of Britain's most successful cultural exports – and the resurgence of Post-Modernism, the favoured style of the developing classes.

The idea that architecture and the creative process are fundamentally about applying order has been challenged by the long-drawn-out death of the Modernist orthodoxy. It is still pervasive, of course, yet various strands of both writing and paper architecture – that is to say the speculative and the unbuilt – are now exploring the avenues opened up by chaos and disorder, creating forms and proposals that draw on devices from literary criticism, cultural theory and social anthropology. Modernism factionalized; today, it encompasses everything from simplistic, single-minded banalities to unimaginative visual shortcuts for luxury and extravagance through to dense, impenetrable academic thought experiments.

By the turn of the 21st century, the average modern architect was avowedly unfamiliar with the everyday and the quotidian, a quality he

or she believed earlier generations had apparently set out to banish. These aspects of life, what the writer and architect Jeremy Till calls the 'contingent', those fundamental yet dull aspects of every project that aren't normally considered as driving factors behind the architectural brief,[7] are precisely the territory in which the New Functionalism exists.

Formalism remains a fertile subject for debate. The houses featured in this book are united by their visual disparity, their forms motivated by expediency, practicality and function. This approach was shared by the original Modernists. 'We know no form problems, only building problems,' Mies van der Rohe wrote in 1923; 'the form is not the goal, but the result of our work. There is no form as such. The really formal is related, connected to the task, the most elementary expression of its solution. Form as a goal is formalism; and this we reject.'[8]

Mies himself claimed to eschew formal relationships between his various projects, a theoretical stretch that critics of the International Style – and there were many – would have been quick to decry. The influence of the masters of the International Style may have been far-reaching and Le Corbusier, Walter Gropius and Mies van der Rohe were indeed heralded like prophets. Nevertheless, the High Modernist years soon gave way to a certain sense of *déjà vu*. 'At Yale,' wrote Tom Wolfe, 'the students gradually begun to notice that everything they designed, everything the faculty members designed, everything that the visiting critics (who gave critiques of student designs) designed ... looked the same. Everyone designed the same ... box ... of glass and steel and concrete, with tiny beige bricks substituted occasionally. This became known as The Yale Box. [...] ... nobody could design anything *but* Yale Boxes.'[9] The artist Saul Steinberg infamously depicted one of the sleek new boxes of glass and steel with a rectangle of blank graph paper, pasted on to one of his spidery cityscapes. Steinberg knew the genre all too well – his adoptive New York had become a stylistic battleground, as the International Style slabs superseded the decorative and artistic flourishes of the first great era of skyscraper building. Functionalism was allied with formal sterility.

One psychological casualty of Modernism's perpetual search for a new domestic architecture was the archetypal image of the house, the pitched-roof vernacular object that proved especially hard to eradicate from the collective psyche. Le Corbusier's *5 Points d'Une Architecture Nouvelle* of 1926 specifically cited the flat roof and the roof garden as an integral element of the house, a means of reclaiming lost space, increasing density and, presumably, improving access to health-giving sun and air. As a result, the definition of 'good architecture' shied away from this universal typology form of the house, preferring to use functionalist justifications for Modernism's abstracted formalism. In other words, simply following the pitched-roof aesthetic demonstrated both a lack of imagination and a commitment to conventional systems. Only by subverting this form – in whatever way possible – is it possible to create a new architecture representative of social and technological progress.

Unsurprisingly, many of the projects featured here attempt to break out of the conventional 'house' form, even subverting it. Yet there are strong psychological bonds with the traditional. In Germany, the domestic archetype is known as *Haus vom Nikolaus*, the house of Santa Claus, and represented by a simple eight-line diagram of a pitched-roof structure that can be rendered without lifting the pen from the page. Thus the domestic can be swiftly and emotionally described in a visual shorthand that is understood from childhood onwards.

01

01
HERZOG & DE MEURON'S
RUDIN HOUSE, LEYMEN,
FRANCE (1997)

02
GLENN MURCUTT'S
SIMPSON-LEE HOUSE
IN MOUNT WILSON,
AUSTRALIA (1994)

02

01

02

03

Once denounced as an archaic throwback, the pitched roof is being reasserted as a progressive device. Herzog & de Meuron's 1997 Rudin House (also known as Project 128) demonstrated that the pitched roof could be deployed as a formal acknowledgment of the immediate past, not merely as pastiche, while the various domestic suburban projects of such architects as Sergison Bates and Lynch Architects use pitched roofs as a logical, pragmatic, functional device, not as a statement of formal eccentricity. Within this book, projects as disparate as Broekx-Schiepers' Lenaerts-Thijs House in Belgium (see p. 122), Titus Bernhard's 9x9 House in Germany (see p. 140) and the Casa en el Campo in Mallorca (see p. 78) by Juan Herreros Arquitectos reference vernacular forms without recourse to imitation or parody.

From the evidence of the following case studies, New Functionalism is a movement without style, a conscious expression of the essential, above self-conscious vanity or expression. Perhaps this is a product of functionalism's apparent lack of concrete definition, a word adrift in architectural history to serve whatever purpose was demanded of it.

The constant mutations of the meaning of functionalism throughout the centuries have been many and contradictory. Before attempting to identify the role of 'function' in the contemporary architectural landscape, it seems imperative to redefine functionalism. The word's journey has been associated with several, often extreme, positions, from lush aesthetic approaches that combine both utility and ornament, to strict militant rules banishing any sort of architectural embellishment in function's sublime presence, and even function's total dismissal – extending even to mockery – by the Post-Modernist approach.

The houses contained in this book reference the many facets of functionalism, many different styles, typologies and approaches, making a mathematically precise definition unfeasible, if not entirely irrelevant. As a result, the idea of a 'new functionalism' is not confined to a single typology and aesthetic. Instead, what emerges from collating projects that share theoretical common ground is that there are only fragments of shared aesthetic and/or technical elements. New Functionalism's visual disparity is an integral part of its being.

This disparity is a deliberate counterpoint to modern culture, in which we have been trained to recognize and categorize almost everything by appearance. The New Functionalism grows stronger by shouting calmly against an easily definable aesthetic. It pushes away from a common visual appearance, a universally acceptable choice of shape or material and a unified style among its representatives. The tendency is not at all arbitrary, borrowing elements from different architectural philosophies and negating others, shaping them into a new movement that reflects the zeitgeist of the 21st century.

Functionalism, when it first appeared in Modernist and later Brutalist form, was set in opposition to structurally unnecessary decoration, designing according to the mantra of 'form following function', dismissing the previous decoration-heavy styles of Art Nouveau and the historical renaissances. The New Functionalism accordingly makes a case for a new resistance to the status quo, standing in deliberate opposition to current design philosophies and 'trends', perhaps even the idea of very idea of 'trend' altogether.

'Traditional Modernism' is an oxymoronic but essential term that acknowledges that in the contemporary era, any reference to Modernism's abstract, pure aesthetic tendencies are simultaneously *historical* and *modern*. However, traditional Modernism has been slowly losing meaning in the face of the increasing new design plurality. As a result, the demand for perfection and the rejection of the everyday, the casual, and unplanned, as well as modern architecture's often dysfunctional relationship with nature, have all started to feel irrelevant.

The Modernist house represented the heroic apogee of the Modernist movement, a space designed not with comfort and homely warmth in mind but rather as a means of proving the ideal of the house as a 'machine for living', flying the flag for the victory of technology and the pioneering spirit of the early decades of the 20th century. Such houses were also designed for a certain group of people: clients who aspired to the modern way of life, an austere but futuristic combination of art, sport and hygiene.

'Architects have thought that they can literally start from scratch, wipe the table clean and install a new system or structure on the ground. [...] Modernism was a tabula rasa attitude,' Swiss architect Bernard Tschumi said in 1997, talking about the different attitudes that different architects have towards a given site at the beginning of the design process.[10] Modernism's status as a social movement was undermined by its inability to scale up to solve issues of mass housing. The architectural historian Tim Benton summed up the movement's insularity: 'Perhaps the key to understanding the Modernist house is that it was not designed for just anyone. This was an art movement, intended for those who could understand and appreciate it.'[11] Modernism is invariably expressed through grandeur and magnificence, characterized by absolutism, rarely accompanied by modesty and even less by adaptability.

Modernism might be in a slow decline, yet its various strands continue to play a high-profile role in architectural culture, ultimately evolving from an avant-garde movement into a symbol of indulgence, a world of branded designer architecture and nostalgic lavish lifestyles, a polished minimalism that has little more than a cursory aesthetic relationship with the original Modern movement.

In an attempt to distance themselves from both the luxury lifestyle approach of a lucky few and the culture of appearances that has defined certain aspects of architectural creation since the late 1980s and early '90s, the new generation of architects – the 'New Functionalists' – have chosen to move towards an aesthetic underlined by pragmatism and driven by needs other than the desire, fuelled by the explosion in design-centric media, to look impeccably manicured. In contrast, roughness, humility and imperfection are slowly becoming acceptable, both to architects and their clients.

So what does this all mean for architecture? For all its faults, Modernism and many of its transformations represented vision, the hope of and an uncompromising devotion to innovation and imagination, as well as a strong belief in technology's ability to create a better future, combined with simplicity and geometrical elegance. Under the umbrella of Modernism, functionalism represented the future; a physical manifestation of a vision of a world to come.

What is the vision being offered by New Functionalism? Will crude reality, affordability and downright modesty define a characterless architectural future? This book sets out to demonstrate that this will not be the case. The New Functionalist house is very much the house of the present. Realistic, tough and unpretentious, this new generation of residential design is as grounded and as strongly connected to its environment and its chronological, geographical and economical coordinates as it could possibly be. These houses do not lack ideas: instead they indicate a shift in critical and aesthetic focus.

Rather than rebelling against society and prescribing patronizing rules for the 'ideal inhabitation' of architecture, this emerging residential architecture sets out to condemn the perfectionism and authority that characterized the Modern movement and its offspring. Tired of outlining the perfect modern lifestyle and designing the perfect modern architecture to accompany it, many contemporary architects are turning their attention and intention towards the questions of the masses, not the élite, and adopting a more pragmatic approach. The worldwide economic crisis that started in 2008 has pushed these considerations to the forefront of the architectural debate.

Despite this, the contemporary architect remains an uncompromising visionary: the architectural utopia still seems within reach. But the direction has changed. By rejecting the thus far unquestioned power of Modernism, architecture is entering a new era of residential design, involving pragmatism and practicality. Function and a utilitarian approach are being combined with craft, imagination and innovation, producing works that embrace social as well as technological change.

Moreover, New Functionalism is not a movement of exclusion. The male-dominated world of the International Style rendered the modern domestic interior as a stage set for conventional gender roles, calculated and prescribed. The houses shown here include the evidence of human existence and a confirmation that they are not just cold, calculated buildings – machines to live in – but dwellings. They are an expression of the dweller's life rather than expressing the sanitarily clean, masculine interior of the Modernist mind.

The New Functionalist house is more fluid, in textures and design rules. It is impossible to ignore not only the designs themselves but also the fact that this architecture is partly created by women. From Viennese architects PPAG (see p. 118) to Pezo von Ellrichshausen Architects in Chile (see p. 34) and noroof architects in New York (see p. 226), women have a new prominence in contemporary architecture, being an active part of the leading design team and a practice's decision-making. Even the aesthetics of presentation are shifting away from strict rigour; the interiors do not appear perfect. They are more welcoming and less clinical. The human presence is clearly felt.

Philosophically, the idea of functionalism is perhaps allied to phenomenology, the understanding of the world through experience. These are spaces that are defined not by a single photographic image containing no signs of human activity, but by the day-to-day lives that take place within them and the mood they create. The Swiss architect Peter Zumthor has written about such notions as atmosphere, experiential space and architectural mood, as well as the *genius loci*, the 'spirit of the place', in architecture. 'Quality of architecture to me is when a building manages to move me. What on earth it is that moves me? [...] One word for it is atmosphere.' he writes.[12] Others demonstrate a similar concern: 'Occupation or use separates art from architecture. If Art is communication then it can be purely metaphysical. If Architecture is function then it must be physical as well as metaphysical.'[13] Such projects as the Element House by Sami Rintala (see p. 54) or the Silent House by Takao Shiotsuka (see p. 144) illustrate an approach that acknowledges memory and place as integral to their design.

The functionalist approaches chronicled in this book share much common ground with phenomenology: both are seeking to define architecture without resorting to a search for the perfect form and the ideal structure and appearance (unlike the rigid rules of Classicism or even the formal perfectionism sought by Le Corbusier's Modular). The New Functionalism would appear to require a phenomenological approach, a focus on the human element within the building, the aura of domesticity, and shaped by the spirit of place and deeply connected to the practicalities of everyday life and experience.

Ultimately, New Functionalism cherry-picks elements of a number of previous styles and architectural approaches, transferring them into the world and the needs of today. No architectural approach is better suited to a constantly evolving, pluralist world. In a similar vein, the zeitgeist-defying work of Robert Venturi and Denise Scott Brown pushed the limits of architecture and challenged the ideas of modernity, albeit in a very different way. Venturi's *Complexity and Contradiction in Architecture*, published in 1966, outlined his 'gentle' manifesto, making explicit reference to the 'richness and ambiguity of modern experience, including that experience which is inherent in art'. Venturi and Scott Brown playfully appropriated Modernist teachings, adding plurality and experience, setting the first stones of the Post-Modern era in place.

Writings such as Venturi's chronicled the shift from Modernism's socially progressive spirit. 'In the Venturi cosmology, the people could no longer be thought of in terms of the industrial proletariat, the workers with raised fists, engorged brachial arteries, and necks wider than their heads, Marxism's downtrodden masses in the urban slums. The people were now the "middle-middle class", as Venturi called them,' Tom Wolfe wrote in his critical narrative of modern architecture, *From Bauhaus to Our House*, in the 1980s.[14] While New Functionalism embraces Venturi's 'Less is a bore' – a playful response to the Modernist 'Less is more' – it also returns a new layer of inclusion and plurality, as befits the demands and context of the 21st century.

The architectural theorist Charles Jencks has argued that Post-Modernism was the inevitable response to a condition he describes as an 'omnipresent reality, particularly in the West, of networking, social levelling, moral relativism, multiculturalism, global migration and media hype'.[15] New Functionalism undoubtedly shares a cultural, geographical and temporal viewpoint with Post-Modernism, but it is equally important to point out that it is more the product of a post-modern *environment*, a quieter, more considered response to changing cultural conditions, rather than the stylistic volte-face represented by Post-Modern architecture itself. Honesty in the use of materials and the importance of utility, pragmatism, modesty and a realistic down-to-earth approach are the core elements of the New Functionalist agenda.

How do we identify the New Functionalism? First, this is a movement that is in deliberate opposition to fashions, trends and the conventional. It exists at the fringes of the architectural mainstream, in an ongoing discourse unconcerned with the tawdry seduction of the digitally created utopia, but celebrating rather the analogue medium of drawings, models, mock-ups and, most importantly of all, the physical act of building itself. There is a respect for craft, a reverence for simple materials and an understanding of the importance of a sense of place, while remaining intrinsically connected to design and technological innovation. New Functionalist architecture is not an all-encompassing architectural method, a scalable approach that can be applied to everything from chairs to city plans. This is the architecture of the everyday and the immediate, expressed on a graspable, domestic scale.

The houses featured in this book share an unselfconscious aesthetic: not a straightforward visual homogeneity, but a common sensitivity to

02

01

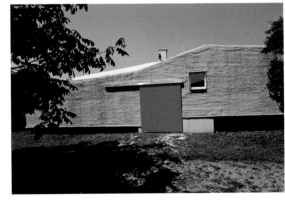

03

04

05

01
LE CORBUSIER'S WORKERS
HOUSING SCHEME LES
QUARTIERS MODERNES FRUGES
IN BORDEAUX, FRANCE (1926)

02
ELEMENTAL'S QUINTA
MONROY PROJECT IN IQUIQUE,
CHILE (2004)

01

02

03

04

05

03
K HOUSE IN HIROSHIMA,
JAPAN, BY FURUMOTO
ARCHITECT ASSOCIATES
(P. 198)

04
HOUSE IN NEWINGTON
GREEN, LONDON, UK,
BY PREWETT BIZLEY
ARCHITECTS (P. 218)

05
LIVE/WORK STUDIO
IN PITTSBURGH,
PENNSYLVANIA, USA, BY
STUDIO D'ARC (P. 230)

place that absorbs vernacular forms and materials as well as the pragmatic desire to extract the most from a site, a brief and a budget. This is architecture that demonstrates a global sensibility, going beyond Critical Regionalism's somewhat self-consciously Modernist legacy and Neo-Classicism and Post-Modernism's shameless quoting of the past or pop culture, to forge an aesthetic and philosophy unencumbered by the weight of historical expectations. Above all, functionalism is fluid. There are no true definitions. Unlike the rigid concrete structure that was Le Corbusier's five points, not all the above elements need be present for a house to be said to have a functionalist approach.

The New Functionalist house doesn't fit into any existing narratives of Modernism. It's literally a step back from the myriad forked pathways of movements and -isms that make up the diagram of architectural 'progress'. Instead, these houses are a reaction against dogmatic adherence to any style and theory.

The case studies in this book are divided into three elemental contexts – rural, suburban and urban – exploring the ways in which contemporary architects are pushing form, material and plan to create a new residential aesthetic in a variety of circumstances. Having established context as one of the most important elements of the New Functionalist approach, the book looks closely at three key environments as a way of making sense of this architecture and its relationship to place.

The rural house, the residential structure situated in the landscape, still represents an aspirational ideal, a vision cemented by some of the most iconic Modernist houses and continually reinforced by the contemporary architectural press. Yet such a vision is, in most cases, far beyond the means of the average house-buyer. The projects presented here represent many different approaches to the rural site, a plurality of approach that encompasses conventional vernacular forms and techniques as well as more 'iconic' designs. By the turn of the 21st century, 'Modernist' modernism tended towards the grandiose, a luxury style for the super-rich. The 'modern house' was part of a cultural arms race kicked off by the avant garde and ultimately bankrolled by the moneyed classes, leaving the sense of social progress that was once integral to the Modern movement far behind. The New Functionalism reclaims (r)evolution.

The second set of projects featured in this book are constructed in a suburban context, typically seen as a space of convention and conformity with little place for innovation. Arguably, though, the suburban condition is the crucible of New Functionalism, a place where quiet creativity can flourish, away from the contextual complexity of the city and the originality-stifling *carte blanche* of the rural site. Many of the featured projects represent a development of the prevailing suburban context. Broekx-Schiepers' Lenaerts-Thijs House in Belgium (see p. 122), Titus Bernhard's 9x9 House in Germany (see p. 140) and BBM Sustainable Design's Sparrow House in the UK (see p. 172) all share a healthy respect for vernacular form, scale and materials without succumbing simply to copying. Instead, they demonstrate concerns about energy, materials and construction, and bring an experimental spirit back to architectural design.

Contextual design is the natural forte of this new pragmatic approach, an acknowledgment of the jumble of the modern urban environment – the final category. These urban houses no longer belong to any particular movement or style; they represent a modest strand of contextual modern architecture that strives to knit together the urban fabric without pastiche or imitation. In particular, the urban context offers the challenges of the terrace and of the infill. Projects featured here, including Studio D'Arc's Live/Work Studio in Pittsburgh (see p. 230), Furumoto's K House in Japan (see p. 198) and Prewett Bizley Architects' Newington Green House in London (see p. 218), show sympathy to surroundings, historical scale and materials, conveying a tough rigour that refuses to be overshadowed by the past.

The contextual divisions adopted in the book provide a practical organization of the contents, a consistent representation of the approaches and values of New Functionalist design. Context is not the only means of defining these works; it is complemented by many different fields and subcategories, reflecting an inherent variety and a sense of inclusion.

For example, it should be immediately apparent that conversion and refurbishment are inherently functionalist ways of working with architecture, an approach that is not confined to qualified professionals. In his book *On Altering Architecture*, the architect and educator Fred Scott writes how 'the intended fit between function and space can be elusive, unfocused, but the image is vivid, which is a reason why the idea of obsolescence is so uncertain with regard to buildings.'[16] *On Altering Architecture* is a lesson in the value of architectural pragmatism, a chronicle of centuries of evolution in the built environment and the often awkward, violent confrontations between alteration and renewal ushered in by the Modernist era. The archetypal example of this collision is Le Corbusier's scheme of worker housing, Les Quartiers Modernes Fruges at Pessac, near Bordeaux, completed in 1926. This workers' estate was built at the height of the architect's purist phase, all rigorously crisp, geometric façades with the five famous points in full effect. From the moment the new owners walked through their front doors, they began to impose their lives upon the scheme, personalizing, painting and extending the structures with ad-hoc infills and neo-vernacular details.[17]

In many respects, developments in countries without the new tradition of iconic architecture illustrate the gradual emergence of the New Functionalist approach, accommodating both pragmatic technological underpinnings and a focus on conversion and reuse. The Chilean architect Cecilia Puga set out a key reason for the ongoing development of contemporary functionalism in her homeland: 'We have never had access to the type of technology that you do in more developed countries, so we missed certain movements like deconstructivism and the more recent focus on digital technologies. Instead, we've been forced to stick with and develop modernism with more modest construction means and with local materials and labour.'[18] The article continues that 'Chile is where we now look for lessons in context, form and sustainability'.

The Quinta Monroy social housing project in Iquique, Chile (2004) by Alejandro Aravena[19] and Elemental[20] illustrates this well, bearing as it does the spirit of the altered Pessac. Ninety-three houses were arranged in small terraces, with a deliberate void left between each unit for later backfilling by the occupants, according to needs and budgets. The façades and walls were left deliberately plain and unadorned, encouraging owners to paint the houses themselves. In the words of the architects, 'the building had to be porous enough to allow each unit to expand within its structure. The initial building must therefore provide a supporting (rather than a constraining) framework in order to avoid any negative effects of self-construction on the urban environment over time, but also to facilitate the expansion process.'[21]

This is a very modern concern. Whereas demolition and reconstruction was once seen as the only definition of progress, issues of sustainability and community continuity are now driving large-scale reuse projects. Such groups as the Existing Homes Alliance in the UK are pushing to 'transform the … existing housing stock and make it fit for the 21st century.'[22] Functionalism is at the heart of this movement: a desire to maximize the value of existing form. Conversion work is architecture with a suppressed ego; Jonathan Tuckey's Providence Chapel (see p. 104), Jesús Castillo Oli's La Ruina Habitada (see p. 74) and Juan Herreros's Casa en el Campo (see p. 78) all provide a carefully thought-out application of new designs on existing structures, using a lightness of touch that both underlines the original structures' identity while simultaneously updating them into a functional, contemporary whole.

The notion that architects must step back from their traditional role as all-knowing providers of a total, incontrovertible artwork is gathering pace, making self-built projects another vital branch of the debate. In these projects, the functionally attuned architect is emerging as a facilitator, fully aware that a signed-off building is not a fixed, eternal sculptural object but a starting point, a blank canvas upon which an occupant can – and should – have an impact. So-called DIY architecture has been regarded as something of an oxymoron by the mainstream architectural profession. The 1970s fashion for self-building and 'community architecture' was branded, rightly or wrongly, by its association with left-wing politics and alternative lifestyles. Yet there are clearly economic as well as aesthetic benefits to stepping back from the conventional systems of design, procurement and construction, an approach that is sympathetic to New Functionalism. Dominic Stevens's own house in Ireland (see p. 50), Casey Brown Architecture's Permanent Camping structure in Australia (see p. 26) and the Single-Family House in the Czech Republic by Kamil Mrva Architects (see p. 128) are all examples of the expedience of the contemporary self-build sensibility.

The work in this book is also about the *process* of architecture, with all its mess and confusion and contradiction and the way in which conversations with materials continue long after a building is supposedly 'finished'. Inspiration and design development are an invaluable part of the identity of each project, hinting at the design to come and setting out the architects' way of thinking, unfolding their methods. This is why so many sketches, tests, study drawings and models are featured in this book. Hand-drawn work and hands-on studies reveal something of the architect's own character, while at the same time they often underline the role of function in the architect's thought processes. Ultimately, the concept sketch and the working model – though often aesthetically pleasing in isolation – have a fundamental and indispensable functional role. Often the first scribbles on a piece of napkin enclose the true essence of a design, assisting with the translation of abstract notions about sense and atmosphere into real buildings.

This is not a scientific functionalism, devoid of humanity, but rather the opposite, a functionalism that embraces the paradoxes and complexities of everyday life and attempts to express these honestly through architecture. As a result, there is no homogeneity, no uniformity or enforced conformity. However, what we do find is the desire for authenticity, a backlash against the computer-generated unbuilt realm of rendered cityscapes and fantasy houses that increasingly populates our minds. It has never been easier to 'build', and virtual proposals crowd the architectural press, their undeniably seductive presentation elbowing the built reality off the pages. This book is a reaction to the computer's role as the cuckoo in the nest: rather than embrace self-conscious

complexity, these are projects that view abstraction as a necessary side-effect of simplicity.

On the other hand, while iconistic architecture has apparently benefited most of all, with the digital design revolution turning the solid form into a plastic fantasy object of limitless potential, functionalism can also revel in this aesthetic freedom. Lopped-off volumes, created almost randomly, virtually by the intersection of two points on a flat plane before being extruded or clipped, have revolutionized the perception of space. In New Functionalist design, simplicity and abstraction are able to come from a different starting point from that of iconic form-making. Even though there may not be a uniformity and conventionality of surface and shape, there is always a pragmatic explanation behind the houses' final abstract form.

The down-to-earth approach, DIY and simplification have had an effect on aesthetics, one that has not been limited to purely functionalist design. A post-industrial picturesque has emerged, running in parallel to the work shown in the book. Sharing the same moral opposition to stylistic slickness, this genre in photography and in fine art seeks to convert decay, spoil, deprivation and strict economical pragmatism of form into a new form of landscape, epitomized perhaps by the Düsseldorf School of Photography – students who studied under Bernd and Hiller Becher, best known for their photographic records of industrial structures. As the Bechers and their followers have demonstrated, there is a certain romance in the studied blankness of derelict architecture, in ruined or abandoned spaces: a romance that can be translated into an architectural approach. The memory of forms and functions not only lingers in a converted space, but also manifests itself in the willingness of the New Functionalism to embrace a particular function, a spatial configuration, a material roughness or even a view from a window.

Craft is another element to consider. Finishes and quality can vary wildly as architects demonstrate a tacit acknowledgment of the death of the modern craft tradition, together with a realization of the beauty of low-cost design and of the fact that high technology materials require specific handling. Such examples as the Portuguese Casa em Azeitão by Atelier Central Arquitectos (see p. 66), or Studiohouse by Degelo Architekten in Büsserach, Switzerland (see p. 160), show a tendency towards a functional abstraction, with materials reduced to their essence and then expressed with care.

The shift towards a more pragmatic modernism has been enhanced by the increased focus on hitherto little-known and smaller-scale (albeit numerous) architectural cultures. The Internet has expanded our design horizons, creating an insatiable demand for visual innovation. This ostensibly superficial fascination with novelty has also revealed a broad disparity in working methods: 'contemporary' architecture has myriad definitions.

Digital technologies have been involved in the evolution of contemporary architecture in more ways than one. Architecture's endless metamorphoses and Modernism's journey have been clearly, loyally and meticulously portrayed by the media – even more so through the ever-growing field of online architectural coverage. A sizeable quantity of modern architecture being produced today is being published, and criticised, via the Internet. The visually dramatic rises to the top.

As a consequence, there are emerging downsides to this totality of architectural awareness. Today, the propagation of architecture is universal. 'Classic' Modernism has never been more popular. Projects

01
PROVIDENCE CHAPEL,
COLERNE, UK, BY JONATHAN
TUCKEY DESIGN (P. 104)

02
LA RUINA HABITADA BY
SPANISH ARCHITECT JESÚS
CASTILLO OLI (P. 074)

03
BERND AND HILLA BECHER,
GRAIN ELEVATOR,
BEAUMETZ, AMIENS, FRANCE,
2000, BLACK-AND-WHITE
PHOTOGRAPH

02

01

03

04

04
STEVENS HOUSE IN IRELAND
BY DOMINIC STEVENS
ARCHITECT (P. 050)

05
PERMANENT CAMPING
PROJECT IN AUSTRALIA BY
CASEY BROWN ARCHITECTURE
(P. 026)

06
SINGLE-FAMILY HOUSE
IN THE CZECH REPUBLIC
BY ARCHITECT KAMIL
MRVA (P. 128)

05

06

01

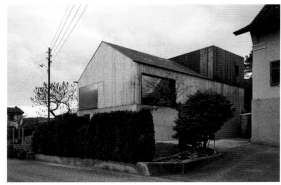

02

03

04

05

06

are instantly discussed around the world, disseminated by blogs and online magazines, with their print counterparts following with lavish coverage only a few weeks behind. Exclusivity has vanished. Scholarship is minimal. Image is everything. The unashamed expectation of instant and omnipresent results and recognition has raised the volume level; new architecture is shouting to be heard above the noise.

With every project distilled down to five or six really good photographs, the media bulldozer can then relentlessly push contemporary design. Photography helped to shape Modernism, and as a result, the modern architect became ever more dependent on the distillation of his or her approach down to a single image: a flat representation of 3D space that can be distributed electronically and reproduced endlessly.

For the first time in Modernism's history, contemporary architecture is not only widely sought out and meticulously presented, but also re-presented, again and again, establishing a popular meritocracy of what is good, what is bad, and what is indifferent. Inevitably, this induces a ruthless invasion of marketing and the strategies of representation. Not everyone is happy. Peter Zumthor argues: 'I think it is important to be genuine, in a world where communications advisors put up facades ... I don't know how long we can go on with artificiality. At certain schools, some students say: "Yeah, I've been trained. Not only to design, but also in marketing and selling myself." It's ridiculous. People are not stupid enough to fall for masquerades.'[23]

The way in which flexibility and aesthetics relate to function and the new have also been considered in myriad ways. One contemporary architect concerned with the shifting perception of the adaptability, utility and aesthetics over the decades is Charles Jacob, a partner in FAT (fashion, architecture, taste). Jacob points out that few practices demonstrate the ideological collision at the heart of late 20th-century British architecture better than Farrell Grimshaw, the short-lived collaboration between Terry Farrell and Nicholas Grimshaw (both partners leaving to set up their own internationally successful studios, gaining knighthoods in the process). 'For Grimshaw, [flexibility] meant buildings that were literally flexible; sophisticated mechanisms that could move and change over time. The Grimshaw camp within the partnership developed a sequence of supposedly repeatable and adaptable metal-framed office buildings. Farrell's notion of flexibility was less aesthetically driven. He was interested in adaptable buildings too, but crucially it was the people and the function that could change, rather than the buildings themselves.'[24]

Similar interpretations of adaptability and function, heavily linked in the past to technology, industrial construction and production speeds, also gave birth to the idea of the prefabricated house. The 'instant architecture' of the house-as-machine depended on the factory system being taken in hand by architects and production directed towards innovation and efficiency. This has been the underlying methodology of the burgeoning modernist prefab movement, although modern prefab is a combination of craft tradition and evolved, bespoke (not mass) production. As far back as 1935, Walter Gropius wrote that 'we are approaching a state of technical proficiency when it will become possible to rationalize buildings and mass-produce them in factories by resolving their structure into a number of component parts. Like boxes of toy bricks, these will be assembled in various formal compositions in a dry state'.[25]

In the modern era, the benefits of the factory-made component have been funnelled into propagating the neo-vernacular, propping up the existing system of house building and marketing. The new iteration of functionalism takes a more off-the-shelf approach. As projects such as the Big Dig House (see p. 180) and the Stevens House (see p. 50) demonstrate, there is still great scope to incorporate standardized and recycled industrialized components into domestic architecture. The idea of reuse continues to flourish in even more ways, as showcased by other examples, including Andrade Morettin's House RR in Brazil (see p. 30) and UNI Architects' house complex in Massachusetts (see p. 176). The use of technology, prefabrication and reused materials in these projects goes hand in hand with a key component of the modern architectural debate: sustainability. The pressing need for low-energy buildings brings innovation back in the service of architecture, adding a further layer to the contemporary meanings of function.

The book also presents works that have been designed as a response and not as a burden to their environments – such as Jomini Zimmermann and Thomas Jomini's Faraday House in Berne (see p. 168) – and not just from an aesthetic angle or by means of layout and orientation. These projects treat architecture as an integral part of nature, attempting to work with their surroundings as complementary and responsive organisms rather than as arrogant conquerors. New Functionalist houses can be modest and simple, not merely because of their occasionally limited budgets and their economically challenged briefs, but also through sheer respect towards natural sustainability and a newly important green sensibility.

Is there opposition to New Functionalism? Not everyone is sympathetic to the idea of a return to architectural simplicity. Peter Cook, writing in *The Architectural Review*, described the British Pavilion at the 2008 Venice Biennale as 'taking seriousness to a new dimension of Cromwellian piety ... a show of quite deliberate interpretational mannerism ... a show of Puritan zeal'.[26] Cook, a practitioner and theorist associated with the playful intersection of pop culture and technology, objected to the unspoken piety and disdain that he felt was encapsulated in the aesthetic of the British Pavilion's participants – Sergison Bates, Tony Fretton, de Rijk Marsh Morgan, Haworth Tompkins – likening the 'stripped-down presentation' of the selected projects to the 'architecture of Fascist Italy'. Cook had perhaps objected to humourlessness. The 2008 British Pavilion broke with the Biennale tradition of presenting the spectacular and the fantastical, instead showcasing a series of housing projects, selected by Ellis Woodman, under the banner 'Home/Away'. The emphasis on domestic and international housing highlighted differences and discrepancies, but above all, it represented a spirited revival of the Smithsons' utopian ad-hocism, and the challenge of bringing true domesticity to contemporary housing design.

So was the return to strict functionalism – almost a new austerity – presented in the 2008 British Pavilion a deliberate return to simplicity and purity with cultural and moral integrity at its heart? Cook presented the 2008 British Pavilion as being representative of a period of 'tedium and architectural whinge' on the country's architectural scene. 'Thank God,' he concluded, 'that history suggests these periods are usually followed by a moment of Great British Invention and playfulness.'

At the heart of this critique of perceived boredom and creative stability is a feeling that strict, unadorned functionalism somehow does the Modernist project a disservice, running counter to a deeply ingrained trust in the importance of a visually articulated progression. The projects in this book attempt to challenge this preconception.

Studied ordinariness certainly need not preclude craft. Many of the featured projects in this book value the role of the craftsman as equal to that of the architect; for example Pezo von Ellrichshausen's Casa Fosc (see p. 34), with its rough-surfaced and tinted concrete façade, or Caruso St John's Brick House (see p. 210), with its sepulchral but beautiful brickwork. The absence of craft is often lamented in contemporary culture. 'Whatever happened to craft?' asked the writer Jonathan Glancey in early 2009, speculating a return to the subject in architectural education, also stressing the way in which 'craft skills, an appreciation of materials, of how things are put together, of how they endure (or not), of how weather affects buildings, and of how architecture is as much a sensual and tactile art and discipline as it is a way of designing buildings and ordering the world we inhabit … would benefit our buildings and townscapes immensely.'[27]

Craft had also been integral to several of the New Functionalism's source movements and above all to Brutalism, albeit craft on an industrialized scale: 'the marks of concrete shuttering were left on the surface, showing the imprint of manual labour.'[28] This was a form of craft that was all too easy to overlook, even to denigrate, especially as the machined slickness of the pop era turned the mass-produced consumer good into the new aspirational object, for architects and shoppers alike. Even the Smithsons, once so attuned to the connection between architecture, art and life, appeared to detach themselves from gritty reality with their 1956 House of the Future, shown at that year's Ideal Home Show, a wipe-clean plastic pod that seemed to equate the disordered imperfection of the human touch with domestic drudgery.

The New Functionalism's appearance today is not irrelevant to such industrial developments or coincidental to the contemporary economic situation. It is a reflex architectural response to mass culture, just as the Smithson's 'discovery of the ordinary' coincided with the dawn of consumer culture and a need to highlight the prosaic over the fantastic.

Ultimately, functionalism is a title that can be tailored for each generation that applies it. For the Modernists – Tom Wolfe's 'Great Whites' – it denoted the scientific application of new building technology, new material and new spatial planning, banishing the old orders to create an architecture that idolized the mechanized efficiency of the production line and the health-giving properties of space, natural light and fresh air and, ideologically, if not literally, turned the house into a machine.

But these are old arguments. Function twisted and turned throughout the 20th century, as backlashes rose and fell and the ideal of use and efficiency continued to mutate along its journey towards the 21st century. The New Functionalism gives a new meaning to progress, gazing upon the architectural world with a steady, newly found – yet thoroughly realistic – optimism. New Functionalism demonstrates a pellucid approach, disavowing the pretensions of what could be termed 'literary architecture' towards complexity and obfuscation. It does not renounce its architectural past; it simply offers an alternative and refreshing version of the present, carving a fresh path for a new, hopeful and global future for contemporary design.

ENDNOTES

1   Louis Sullivan, 'The Tall Office Building Artistically Considered', Lippincott's Magazine, no. 57, March 1896, pp. 403–409

2   Quoted in The Architectural Review, December 1936, from writings in 1920

3   See Paul Virilio, Bunker Archaeology, second edition, Princeton Architectural Press, New York, 2009

4   Owen Hatherley, 'Penthouse and Pavement', The Guardian, 2 May 2009

5   Claude Lichtenstein and Thomas Schregenberger (eds), As Found: The Discovery of the Ordinary, Lars Müller Publishers, Baden, 2001, p. 8

6   Conversation with the authors, 15 May 2008

7   Jeremy Till, Architecture Depends, MIT Press, Cambridge, Massachusetts, 2009

8   Mies van der Rohe, 'Bauen', G2, September 1923, quoted in Dietrich Neumann, 'Three Early Designs by Mies van der Rohe', Perspecta: The Yale Architectural Journal, vol. 27, 1992, pp. 76–97

9   Tom Wolfe, From Bauhaus to Our House, Farrar, Straus and Giroux, New York, 1981

10 Quoted by William Menking in Iain Borden, Joe Kerr, Jane Rendell and Alicia Pivaro (eds), Unknown City: Contesting Architecture and Social Space, MIT Press, Cambridge, Massachusetts, and London, 2002, p. 371

11 Tim Benton, The Modernist Home, V&A Publications, London, 2006

12 Peter Zumthor, Atmospheres, Birkhauser, Basel, 2006

13 From the lecture 'Space: Between Reality and Concept. Making or Shaping Space in the 21st Century', Boyd Cody Architects, quoted on www.boydcody.com

14 Tom Wolfe, op. cit.

15 Charles Jencks, Critical Modernism, Wiley Academy, London, 2007

16 Fred Scott, On Altering Architecture, Routledge, London, 2008, p. 5

17 Philippe Boudon, Lived-in Architecture: Le Corbusier's Pessac Revisited, Lund Humphries, London, 1972

18 Cecilia Puga, quoted in 'Chile', Jaffer Kolb and Patricio Mardones, The Architectural Review, June 2009, p. 40

19 www.alejandroaravena.com/

20 www.elementalchile.cl/

21 www.elementalchile.cl/category/vivienda/iquique/

22 www.existinghomesalliance.net/resources.php

23 Peter Zumthor, interview by Rob Gregory, The Architectural Review, May 2009, p. 20

24 The Odd Couple, blog post 28 February 2009, fantasticjournal.blogspot.com/2009/02/odd-couple.html

25 Walter Gropius, The New Architecture and the Bauhaus, Faber and Faber, London, 1935, p. 39

26 Peter Cook, 'Let's be serious – let's be dogmatic', The Architectural Review, November 2008, p. 28

27 Jonathan Glancey, 'Whatever happened to craft?', Building Design, 27 March 2009

28 Owen Hatherley, op. cit.

01

02

01
THE BRITISH PAVILION
AT THE 2008 ARCHITECTURE
BIENNALE IN VENICE

02
INTERIOR OF BRICK HOUSE,
LONDON, BY CARUSO ST JOHN
(P. 210)

Rural

Agricultural buildings were once considered one of the primary visual and technical sources of Modern architecture. The great grain elevators of the American Midwest thrilled the early Modernists with their sheer scale and their blank, abstract forms, while the farm buildings at Gut Garkau near Lübeck, designed by the German architect Hugo Häring in the mid-1920s, are regarded as the epitome of form following function: a mixture of organic forms arranged in utter subservience to the prosaic daily routine of a herd of dairy cows.

Somewhere along the way, the rough functionalism of agricultural construction gave way to a more anonymous, off-the-shelf aesthetic, which was as bereft of individual expression as the anonymous systems-built apartments and office blocks of the post-war era. The influence of the barn and the silo also began to wane. The fashion for barn conversions, reflecting as it did the swift erosion of small-scale farming, created a new building form, one that combined the expansive interior of the warehouse with collected remnants of a former life – a pulley, exposed beams, sundry pieces of ironwork – displayed like totems of an earlier age.

Casey Brown Architecture's Permanent Camping project, completed in 2007, is a return to the swift expediency of agricultural and industrial design. While the project's name alludes to its playful mix of tent and cabin, in form and materials it owes everything to economic and functional necessity. Located in Mudgee County, New South Wales, this 3 x 3 metre (10 x 10 foot) retreat is intended for just one or two people.

Sitting atop a ridge, Permanent Camping forms a miniature landmark in this sparse landscape: the expansive views from the structure are punctuated by 'ancient dead trees' and lumps of granite. Robert Brown and Caroline Casey's architectural response is suitably tough; this is an entirely self-contained, off-grid structure, and the corrugated-metal circular rainwater-collection tank joins the main structure to form a solemn composition of monolith-like forms. A two-storey hardwood frame is clad in corrugated copper, with a system of folding panels to open up the ground floor to the boulder-strewn surroundings or close it completely against the elements.

Functionalism is reclaimed for a domestic purpose, albeit an ascetic one.

Rural | PERMANENT CAMPING
Casey Brown Architecture
Australia

Rural | PERMANENT CAMPING
Casey Brown Architecture
Australia

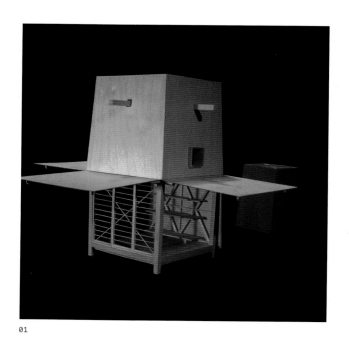

01

02

01–03
AN EARLY WOODEN MODEL
OF THE HOUSE, SHOWING
THE SHUTTERS IN OPEN
AND CLOSED POSITIONS,
ALONG WITH A SCULPTURAL
METAL MAQUETTE

04
THE STRUCTURAL TIMBER
FRAME BEING PREPARED
IN THE WORKSHOP

05
SETTING OUT THE HOUSE'S
COMPACT SQUARE FOOTPRINT

06
PERMANENT CAMPING WAS
CONSTRUCTED AND ERECTED
IN THE WORKSHOP BEFORE
BEING DISMANTLED AND
TAKEN TO SITE

04

05

06

03

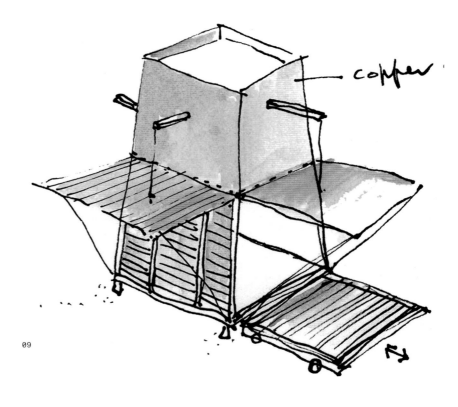

09

07

08

<u>07</u>
THE FRAMING UNDER
CONSTRUCTION

<u>08</u>
THE FRAMING GOES UP
ON SITE

<u>09</u>
EARLY CONCEPT SKETCH,
WITH PROPOSED SLIDE-OUT
DECK ARRANGEMENT

OPPOSITE
HOUSE RR SET WITHIN ITS
RICH GREEN SURROUNDINGS

RIGHT
THE HOUSE'S LONG
FAÇADES COMPLETELY
OPEN UP, UNITING
INSIDE AND OUTSIDE

Rural | HOUSE RR
Andrade Morettin Arquitetos
Brazil

Brazilian architects Vinicius Andrade and Marcelo Morettin understand from experience that it is important to design with a sense of place in mind, an approach that saves time as well as money. This design methodology has been the practice's tool of choice on many projects. When Andrade and Morettin began the House RR (2007), a holiday retreat in the Atlantic rainforest of Itamambuca on the north coast of the state of São Paulo, the sense of place shaped the design.

Commissioned by a young couple seeking an environmentally friendly holiday house, the building was planned on a minimal budget. House RR is located in a beautiful spot surrounded by dense vegetation, only a few metres away from the sea. Unfortunately, this means that it is also subjected to the hot and extremely humid climate of the forest. Because of being subject to extremes of climate, the building shell had to provide not only a welcoming home but also protection from the intense sun, frequent rain, high temperatures and numerous insects.

Creating protection did not just mean keeping nature and the elements out, but also working with the climate in order to make the most of the natural resources. For example, the ocean and forest views were critical in the house's design, and the welcoming sea breeze, combined with the building's clever open-plan layout, ensures permanent natural cross-ventilation. The house is raised 75 centimetres (30 inches) above the ground to facilitate this, with the structure's roof reaching an airy 6 metres (20 feet) high. Two long side façades clad in transparent screen panels can be completely opened up to the scenery.

The house demands minimal energy consumption for operation and maintenance, and was designed to be able to accommodate photovoltaic panels on the roof. Additionally, the generous openings allow natural light into the interior during the day without need of artificial support. This contributes to the building's passive-energy sustainable approach, while avoiding expensive green technologies.

House RR's green approach is also based on its 'lightness' in material use. The main materials used are simple and functional: wood for the timber frame; steel, galvanized for the joints and with EPS (expanded polystyrene) filling for the cladding; and concrete for the foundation pillars, which hold the building above ground. Glass-fibre screens with PVC coating cover the residence's large side openings, to protect from mosquitoes without standing in the way of the beautiful views. All the construction elements were prefabricated, saving both time and money for the clients, and also minimizing waste and the construction site's overall environmental impact.

Andrade Morettin consider the house as part of the practice's ongoing research into developing appropriate solutions to Brazil's housing problems, confidently seeing a practical architectural approach as the best response to local geographical and socio-economic conditions. Their aim was to create a prototype, which could ultimately be used en masse to provide a cheap and easy-to-construct architectural solution for regions with a similar climactic context.

Rural | HOUSE RR
Andrade Morettin Arquitetos
Brazil

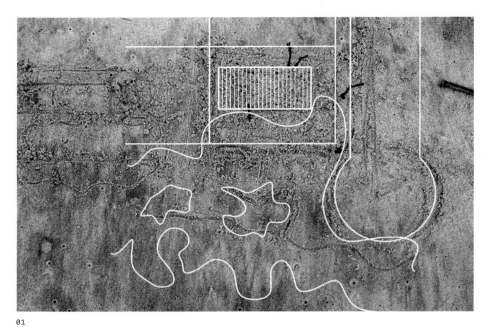

01

02

<u>01</u>
HOUSE RR SITE-PLAN SKETCH

<u>02</u>
ONE OF ANDRADE MORETTIN'S
PRELIMINARY STUDY MODELS

<u>03-04</u>
THE HOUSE'S GROUND-
AND FIRST-FLOOR
PLANS, SHOWING THE
OPEN-PLAN LAYOUT

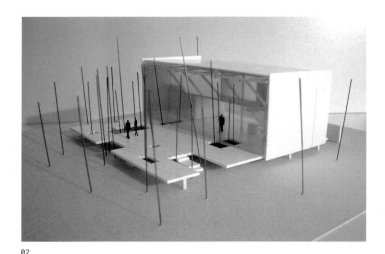

03

04

05

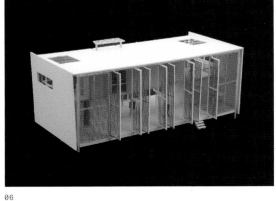

06

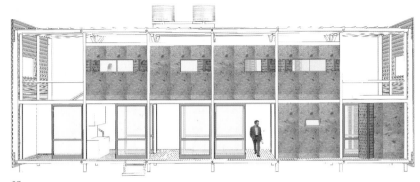

07

<u>05</u>
HOUSE RR'S CROSS-SECTION

<u>06</u>
THE PROJECT'S FINAL MODEL

<u>07</u>
THE HOUSE'S LONG SECTION
SHOWN IN PERSPECTIVE

Rural | CASA FOSC
Pezo von Ellrichshausen Architects
Chile

OPPOSITE
THE HOUSE'S LARGE WINDOWS
OFFER LONG VIEWS THROUGH
THE NEARBY TREES

THIS PAGE
THE GREEN-TINTED SINGLE
VOLUME OF FOSC SITS ON
THE PLOT'S HIGHEST POINT

Rural | CASA FOSC
Pezo von Ellrichshausen Architects
Chile

01   02   03

Chilean practice Pezo von Ellrichshausen is best known for the widely published Casa Poli (2005), a concrete house on a dramatic site that was one of the high-profile projects ushering in a new era for contemporary Chilean architecture. Since then the small practice headed by Mauricio Pezo and Sofia von Ellrichshausen has completed several more designs, focusing on modest scale, simple materials and straightforward planning.

The small but beautiful Casa Fosc is situated on the Venado road on the way to the city of San Pedro, south of Santiago. When the architects began the project in 2007, they were given a very dense programme for a buildable area of 160 square metres (1720 square feet). The brief outlined a house for an art-loving family of no fewer than six, so the requirements included a large number of bedrooms (at least five) and bathrooms.

Apart from the challenges of working with the intense programme, the architects also had to accommodate the prospect of a possible future division of the site into smaller parts. As a result, they chose to assemble everything in a single volume, located at the highest point of the 597 square metre (6426 square foot) inclined plot. Positioning the house at the top of the site not only left the rest of the land free for future sharing, but also created open views far beyond the site and its high trees.

The house itself is a simple prismatic-shaped volume on three levels, featuring large solid exterior walls and a carefully planned interior circulation system – a vertical shaft in the building's main structural core, which holds a steel and wooden stair and threads through all the main areas, making long corridors redundant. The more private rooms are located in the first and third levels, while the second floor is designated as the social part of the house. This is also the floor that connects naturally to the ground level outside.

Construction was completed in 2009. The reinforced-concrete structure was treated with a waterproof copper oxide wash that gives the house a green patina, contrasting with the aluminium window frames. Internally, the shuttered concrete is painted. Wood interior finishes, as well as wooden and stone floors, were also used. The openings respond directly to the internal layout's needs as well as to the orientation and vistas, at the same time elegantly breaking up the density of these massive walls. The walls – a sandwich construction of two concrete slabs and an in-between insulation layer – were poured *in situ*.

The monolithic building was inspired by local old rusted square pedestals, which have an appearance that seems at the same time man-made and natural – a series of objects introduced to the architects by the art-admiring clients. Its realization, however, was dictated largely by the practical present and future needs of the large household. The structure may follow the owners' and architects' symbolic and aesthetic vision, but its materials and internal layout also represent the most cost- and spatially efficient way to make a busy family home work in perfect harmony.

01
THE MAIN STAIRCASE
FEATURES WOODEN STEPS

02
CLEVER VERTICAL PLANNING
TRANSFORMS THE LAYOUT'S
ODD SHAPES INTO
COMFORTABLE LIVING SPACES

03
THE ARCHITECTS HAVE
EXPLOITED THE LIMITED
INTERIOR SPACE TO
THE FULL

06

04

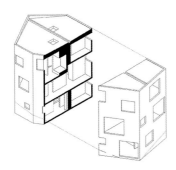

05

Rural | FOSC HOUSE
Pezo von Ellrichshausen Architects
Chile

07

09

07
PRELIMINARY SKETCH OF
CASA FOSC

08-09
THE ARCHITECTS WORKED
ON SEVERAL STUDIES OF THE
INTERIOR SPACE IN ORDER
TO MAKE THE MOST OUT
OF THE INDIVIDUAL ROOMS

10
THE CONCRETE WALLS WERE
POURED IN SITU

11
THE BUILDING OF CASA FOSC

12
LIVING AREA STUDY SKETCH

13
THE FAÇADE IS DYED
GREEN WITH A COAT
OF COPPER OXIDE

10

11

12

13

Rural | MAISON À 100,000 EURO
Beckmann-N'Thépé
France

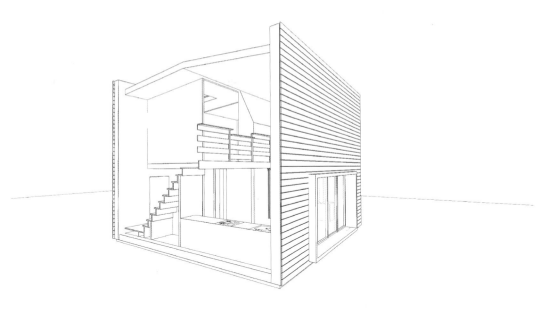

This proposal for an ultra-modest house, put forward in 2009, comes from a firm of architects better known for larger-scale projects. Aldric Beckmann and Françoise N'Thépé have collaborated since 2001, working on commercial and residential projects, as well as representing France in the International Biennale of Architecture in Venice. Their work is characterized by a focus on surface and texture, with rich materials being combined with adventurous physical form.

The Maison à 100,000 Euro is a marked departure. Located in Bellaviers, Normandy, the cube-shaped house is an experiment in low-cost construction. The site is bounded by woodland on two sides, with a main aspect towards the west. To the east, a shallow slope overlooks the forest of Bellême. The basic form of the new house derives elements of its proportions from the nearby vernacular, beginning with a solid cube that contains simple subdivisions of internal space to make a double-height living area and two mezzanine-level sleeping platforms, with a shallow pitched roof concealed behind the raised façade.

The façades are clad in a coated and varnished fabric, creating a dark brown patina that is strongly reminiscent of the region's traditional tiled façades. The compact floor plan has resulted in very tight planning, with the wooden construction allowing for a great deal of flexibility and, naturally, keeping costs down to allow this two-to-three-bed structure to come in at an extremely economical price. Another example of an architecture that draws on the pragmatic and direct aesthetic of industrialized agriculture, the house in Bellaviers offers a way forward for low-cost dwellings as a counter to the economic challenges that face rural regions.

Rural | THE BLACK HOUSE
Tank Architectes
France

LEFT
LOCATED ON THE VERY EDGE
OF THE VILLAGE, THE BLACK
HOUSE DRAWS INSPIRATION
FROM INDUSTRIALIZED
AGRICULTURE

RIGHT
THE OPEN-PLAN GROUND-
FLOOR SPACE IS BISECTED
BY A TOP-HUNG STAIRCASE

This angular single-family house, shaped like an irregularly sided octagon, squats on a large backland plot in the small French village of Radinghem-en-Weppes, west of Lille. Overlooking ploughed fields to the east, with the rear façades of the village's main street to the west, the Black House is a stealthy, subtle addition to the rural landscape. Rather than imitate the pitched terracotta roofs of the surrounding villas, Tank Architectes have adapted the aesthetic of the local barns and agricultural buildings – mundane, stock structures for storing machinery and sheltering animals and feed.

Radinghem-en-Weppes is laid out in a linear fashion along the D62 road that runs north–south through the village. Behind the houses fronting the main street are the functional structures that serve local farmers, hidden from view just like this contemporary house. The house, completed in 2006, epitomizes the transfer of technology and aesthetics from modern agriculture to domestic design, and the abandonment of formalism, structured façade, symmetry and pattern.

The Black House also moves on from the imagery and form of the traditional 'great barn', a vernacular form gradually usurped by modern farming methods and either demolished or converted in their thousands to houses during the 1970s and '80s, creating a sub-genre of contemporary residential design in the process. Taking its name from the black corrugated metal cladding that makes the structure a discreet, indistinct presence in its long, narrow plot, tucked out of general sight, the Black House sidesteps the romantic notion of the 'barn conversion'.

The plan places the main living space in a long room at the heart of the house, with a staircase to the north and a kitchen and utility areas arranged in two 'wings' to the east and west. Three bedrooms are placed upstairs, all of which have access to a large west-facing terrace – giving views across the fields – on the roof of the kitchen below. Inside, the finishes are minimal, with floor-to-ceiling partitions used in the main living area to maximize the perception of space. An entrance ramp leads up to the front door in the west façade, while a larger terrace opens off the living area and kitchen to the east.

The Black House is not the first time that Tank Architectes have experimented with traditional and industrial forms. The practice was founded in 2005 by Lydéric Veauvy and Olivier Camus and the small office is based in Roubaix, north-west of Lille. Their other projects have included large-scale housing, urban infrastructure, retail stores and private houses, including the Peniche House, the conversion of an industrial barge to a home, reflecting the architects' interest in domesticating technology.

01

02

01
AN EAST-FACING WOODEN
DECK OPENS OFF THE GALLEY
KITCHEN, OVERLOOKING
OPEN FIELDS

02
THE METAL FAÇADE
IS RIGOROUSLY DETAILED,
MEETING THE GROUND
WITH NO SEAM

03
GROUND-FLOOR PLAN,
ILLUSTRATING THE SERVICES
PUSHED TO THE EDGES, WITH
A LARGE LIVING SPACE AT
ITS HEART

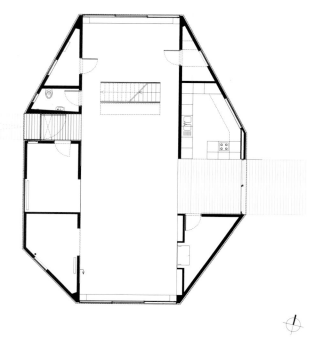

03

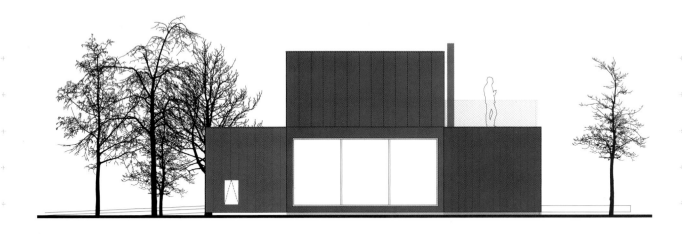

04

05

04
SOUTH FAÇADE:
THE TERRACE OPENS OFF
THE MASTER BEDROOM

05
WEST (ENTRANCE) FAÇADE,
SHIELDED FROM THE VILLAGE
BY TREES

RIGHT
THE MAISON INDIVIDUELLE
MONTBERT IN CONTEXT.
THE GLAZED GARDEN FAÇADE
BRINGS DAYLIGHT INTO
THE WINTER GARDEN AT
THE HEART OF THE HOUSE

This family house in the French village of Montbert was completed in 2006 to designs by the Nantes-based architect Xavier Fouquet. Essentially a modern addition to an ad hoc series of buildings dating from various parts of the last few centuries – an old barn, a late 20th-century villa – the Maison Individuelle Montbert is envisaged as a framework around a predetermined space, pushing the client's available site area to the maximum with a low-cost, simple external fabric.

Fouquet describes the project as having an 'internal logic', with the actual form of the structure arising from the building process itself and from the client's demands and ongoing changes made to the plan throughout construction. 'It is the shape that arises from a negotiation,' he writes, adding that the most crucial aspect is not the physical form of the house, but its relationship with the external space. 'We must think about the relationship between nature and building – nature is a partner for humans.'

In particular, this interplay between structure and landscape shapes Fouquet's views on environmentally friendly building; the architect believes in a 'dynamic relationship with nature', with modern nature itself accepted as a largely fictional creation. Fouquet's desire to accommodate landscape stresses the importance of such figures as the American writer J.B. Jackson, a landscape theorist who published extensively about the impact humankind has on the landscape, and the close relationship between history and geography.

The Montbert house was undertaken in an extempore fashion. 'We work only on plan, with no sketches, no models, and minimal use of computers,' says Fouquet. The wooden structure grew organically out of the site, originally occupied by a small shed and sandwiched between two party walls that stand at 90 degrees to each other. The house is little more than a glass and polycarbonate shell, built around a muscular wooden framework that forms an inside/outside space to bridge the gap between the accommodation and the garden via an internal winter garden.

The materials are economical and hard-wearing and the construction methods traditional. The pine frame structure supports wooden flooring, clad in chipboard and plywood, plus a mixture of clear and opaque ribbed polycarbonate for the side façade and roof. At around 220 square metres (2370 square feet), accommodation is generous, but it is the expansive relationship between internal and external space that really impresses, enhanced by the warmth of the basic materials and the lack of prescriptive, rigorous design. The Maison Individuelle Montbert forms an organic enclosure, modern in form yet traditional in its warm embrace of the surroundings.

Rural | MAISON INDIVIDUELLE MONTBERT
Xavier Fouquet
France

Rural | MAISON INDIVIDUELLE MONTBERT
Xavier Fouquet
France

01

02

03

01
THE SITE BEFORE
CONSTRUCTION BEGAN:
A COLLECTION OF SHEDS
AND LEAN-TOS AT THE REAR
OF AN EXISTING HOUSE

02
THE LIVING ROOM UNDER
CONSTRUCTION, LOOKING
BACK DOWN THE GARDEN

03
THE WOODEN-FRAMED
GLAZED SECTION UNDER
CONSTRUCTION

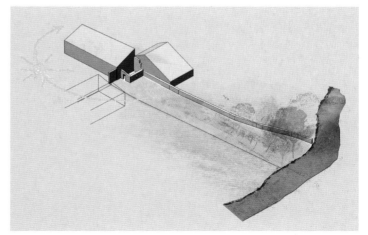

05

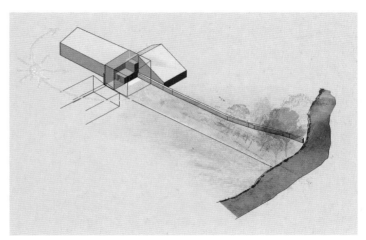

06

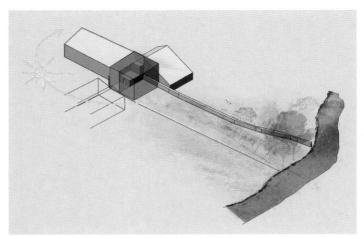

07

04

04
THE REAR FAÇADE UNDER
CONSTRUCTION

05-07
MASSING DIAGRAM
ILLUSTRATING THE
ARRANGEMENT OF HOUSE,
WINTER GARDEN
AND GLAZED ELEMENT

Dominic Stevens built his own house in Ireland at the turn of the century. The structure is a provocation, not aesthetically but economically – a deliberate attempt to undermine a system that Stevens believes locks homeowners into long-term debt in return for a substandard product. The architect explains how he is driving change from within, tracing a problem back to its source so as to prevent undesired consequences. In the case of architecture, the problem in hand is 'bungalow blight', the disparaging term for the quasi-suburban sprawl that has seen parts of post-agrarian Ireland spotted with white-walled, pitched-roof structures, all striving to conform to a mythical ideal of the 'country cottage'.

Stevens and his former partner, the artist Mari-Aymone Djeribi, did much of the building work themselves, beginning by living on the site in 'in tents and temporary structures' so as to 'learn its routes, winds, shelter and views'. The building began as two prefabricated timber boxes, one to live in, one to sleep in, sited so as to make the most of the site and forming the heart of the new house. A timber frame, inspired by the great exponent of self-build architecture, Walter Segal, was combined with an 'earth-bound' structure with thick, rough walls.

The living spaces slot in between the beams as 'two horizontal planes sailing above the landscape', with floor-to-ceiling windows inserted into the timber grid, which was designed specifically to take standard sheets of material. Everything is pared down to the bare minimum. 'The cladding is palette wood: after its five-to-ten-year life span it will be burnt in the stove,

the building getting a fresh skin.' The walled ground-floor space is rougher, more textural. The non-structural insulating walls, built from straw bales rendered with lime plaster, form 'in-between spaces', 'ambiguous spaces waiting to be named, waiting for a pattern of use to settle on them', in keeping with Stevens's slow approach to creating architecture.

The low-technology approach saved money and resulted in a project that has excellent passive heating and ventilation qualities thanks to the south-facing glazing, thick walls and turf roof. For Stevens, the construction process was an important part of the journey. 'In the past in rural Ireland people built their own homes with the help of friends and neighbours. These cottages that they built using simple methods and local materials are now cherished and loved both as homes and as tourist objects, they have entered our psyche as the image of the inviting, warm, comforting home. Nowadays legislation makes it almost impossible to build your house yourself; our economy seems to be more important than our happiness.'

The son of a building contractor, Stevens has created a house that is a deliberate antidote to Ireland's now-evaporated economic dream, when for a few years it was the Celtic Tiger that swept a new developer culture along in its wake. Growing slowly, piece by piece, this is a house at one not just with the landscape, but with the developing needs of its occupiers. 'Building one's own house is a vernacular tradition almost lost in most rural communities in Ireland. It makes dreams obtainable, an empowering yet economically pragmatic experience.'

Rural | STEVENS HOUSE
Dominic Stevens Architect
Ireland

Rural | STEVENS HOUSE
Dominic Stevens Architect
Ireland

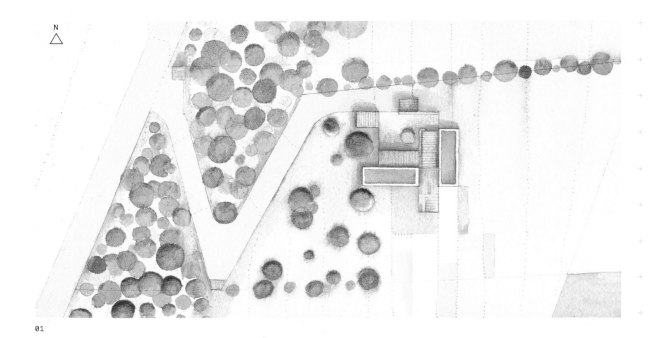

01

01
SITE PLAN, ILLUSTRATING
THE HOUSE'S ORGANIC
GROWTH, WHEELING OUT
FROM A SINGLE STRUCTURE
INTO A COLLECTION
OF LINKED PAVILIONS

02-03
PRELIMINARY DESIGN
SKETCHES

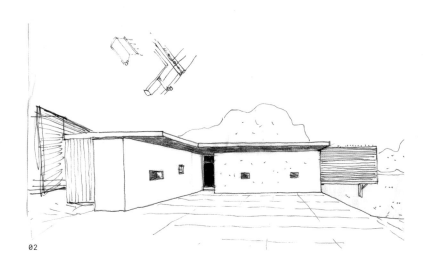

02

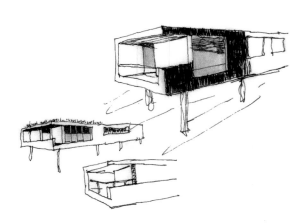

03

04

05

06

07

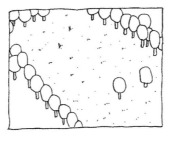
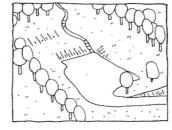

08

04–07
CONSTRUCTION OF THE
WOODEN FRAMING FOR
THE LIVING SPACE

08
THE ARCHITECT'S OWN
SKETCH ILLUSTRATES THE
HOUSE'S CONSTRUCTION
SEQUENCE, WITH ADDITIONAL
ROOMS ADDED OVER TIME

09
DESIGN SKETCH,
STEVENS HOUSE

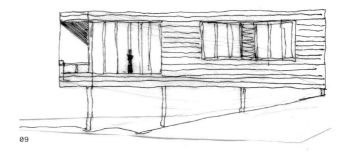

09

Rural | ELEMENT HOUSE
Rintala Eggertsson Architects
South Korea

THIS PAGE
THE ELEMENT HOUSE
IS A COMPOSITION OF
FIVE VOLUMES

OPPOSITE
THE SOIL IN THE
STRUCTURE'S COURTYARD
REPRESENTS THE NATURAL
ELEMENT OF EARTH

Rural | ELEMENT HOUSE
Rintala Eggertsson Architects
South Korea

Even though this project was never meant to be a permanent home, but rather an abstract, house-like installation, it was nonetheless designed to be as close as possible to a fully functioning residence. Its Finnish architect, Sami Rintala, has incorporated the project's locality and history into the design, as well as working with the main principles of conventional house layout.

In 2005, Rintala was invited to take part in the design of a new park in Anyang, a satellite city of South Korea's capital, Seoul. This large-scale project was named Anyang Public Art Park, and the participating artists and architects were all asked to contribute to the conception of a series of art installations and small buildings and pavilions that were spread throughout the landscape.

Faced with a fast-paced South Korean building schedule, Rintala pushed forward with the creation of numerous concept sketches and studies and designed a simple geometrical house, based on the three-dimensional composition of five large cubical spaces – four 3 x 3 x 3 metres (10 x 10 x 10 feet), and one 6 x 6 x 6 metres (20 x 20 x 20 feet). Each cube comprises a separate room. All the smaller boxes were made out of wood, and each connects directly only to the larger main one, clad in rusty steel. The name of the complex – Element House – sprang from the idea that each of the four smaller spaces would be designed to contain one of the four main natural elements; so the attic cube is empty, symbolizing air, while the cellar represents water, the first floor fire, and the courtyard earth.

Completed in 2006, the installation is situated in the park's river valley, at the top of a small wooded hill. Apart from the steel and wood used for the box-shaped rooms, all the other materials were kept to a bare minimum. Foundations and cellar are made from concrete, while safety glass was introduced to cover the openings. Where possible, materials were chosen for their connection to the structure's natural environment, with colours and qualities that imitate the colours and textures of the forest that surrounds the house. Floors are covered in jade and marble gravel, a different type and colour of stone in each room, in response to the surrounding nature's bright greens, browns and greys.

The architect's goal was for the structure to function just like a real house, providing shelter for holiday-makers, travellers and hikers. Historically, this area was filled with traditional temples, as the entire valley was an important Buddhist retreat. The Element House serves as a stopover for rest and relaxation, where guests may enjoy the mountain views and light a stick of incense in memory of the ancient Buddhist traditions.

The Norway-based practice, now called Rintala Eggertsson Architects, is particularly proud of this symbolic house-style project. It is a contemporary structure that remains in harmony with its current surroundings but also evokes memories of the area's former life and use, acting as a housing archetype, an artistic representation of the four basic elements and a resting spot.

the smaller box seems
like resting on top of
the bigger one

01

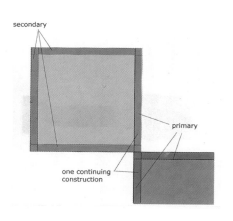

secondary

primary

one continuing
construction

the surfaces are on same level
= even continuation

secondary construction
=the frame of the small box

primary construction continues
in the smaller box

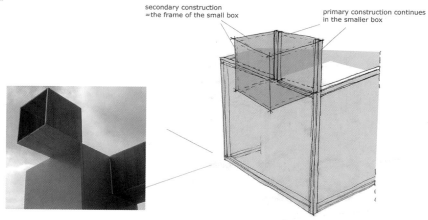

01
THE ARCHITECT'S NOTES ON
THE BUILDING'S STRUCTURE
AND CONSTRUCTION

02

03

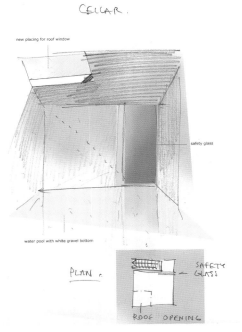

CELLAR.

new placing for roof window

safety glass

water pool with white gravel bottom

PLAN.

SAFETY GLASS

ROOF OPENING

04

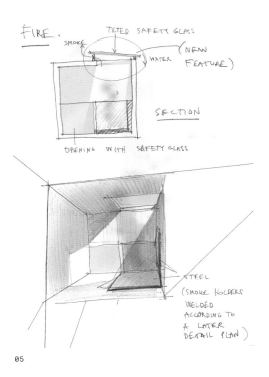

FIRE.

TILTED SAFETY GLASS

SMOKE

WATER

(NEW FEATURE)

SECTION

OPENING WITH SAFETY GLASS

STEEL

(SMOKE HOLDERS WELDED ACCORDING TO A LATER DETAIL PLAN)

05

Rural | CASA TÓLÓ
Álvaro Leite Siza Vieira
Portugal

Looking more like a concrete bunker or abandoned military installation than a house, Tóló House (Casa Tóló) was the creation of Portuguese architect Álvaro Leite Siza Vieira. The holiday home (completed in 2005), located in the North Vila Real District in Lugar das Carvalhinhas, was commissioned in 1999 and evolved into an unusual series of oversized steps, covering a maximum of 180 square metres (1940 square feet), which follow the hill's natural incline.

The project's main characteristic, which largely dictated the house's final form, was the site's particular location; a long, narrow, steep hillside plot. The site's total area was about 1000 square metres (10,760 square feet), and the architect was asked to create a comfortable and modern holiday house, which would include up to three bedrooms, a bathroom, living room, dining room, small kitchen, pantry, and even a small outdoor swimming pool.

The road can be accessed from the top side of the plot, and for practical purposes – such as direct car access – the house's entrance was placed there. A second access, reached through more natural surroundings, was also planned from the south side. The internal layout is clear and follows the external arrangement of interconnected orthogonal volumes. Each one of the boxes houses a separate function, with the living areas placed at the top of the plot and more private spaces at the lower end. While the building's main construction material is raw reinforced PVC-insulated concrete, the interiors are plastered and white-painted, featuring wooden floors, doors and baseboards. External doors and window-frames are metal.

Respecting the area's natural topography, the building was designed around the existing trees, manoeuvring its plan around them. The cascade of roofs forms a series of outsized steps that also act as support-walls for the gardens, mimicking soil-supporting techniques traditionally used around the Mediterranean region. Additionally, taking advantage of the plot's sharp inclination and south-facing orientation, the architect ensured that every single one of the separate linked volumes has access to natural light and open views towards the surrounding forest.

Ecological as much as practical concerns were involved in the decision to half-bury the house in the slope. The gesture ensures thermal insulation and energy sustainability, resulting also in an ongoing economic benefit for the clients. Additionally, the slab-covered volumes enhance the structure's waterproofing.

A network of paths and walkways connects the different levels of the site, the inside and the outside, and the many gardens and patios. These paths are spread across the plot, seamlessly integrated into the overall house's design. The alignment of the exterior steps that march down the site corresponds to the levels of the ceilings within the house. 'This way, the house itself is a path,' says Álvaro Leite Siza Vieira. 'Its form alone organizes a fundamental outdoor route.' Parts of the terrain are covered in reinforced-concrete paving stones, and the roofing is composed of thermal insulation and prefabricated anti-slip tiles.

According to the architects this architecture that is 'neither horizontal, nor vertical' is a directly function-led response to the house's context and the challenges of the location – a geometric, almost modular architecture, highly adaptive to both topology and climate. From a distance it resembles an abstract cascade of rocks falling down the hill.

THIS PAGE
AN EXTERIOR STAIRCASE
CONNECTS THE UPPER LEVELS
WITH THE LOWER ONES

OPPOSITE
THE ROOFS' OVERSIZED
'STEPS' CORRESPOND TO THE
LEVELS OF THE CEILINGS
WITHIN THE HOUSE

Rural | CASA TÓLÓ
Álvaro Leite Siza Vieira
Portugal

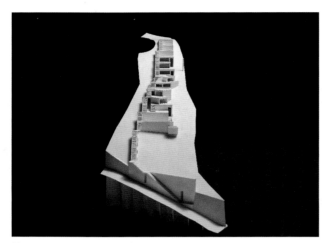

01

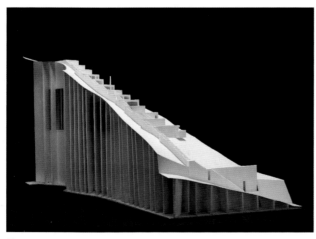

02

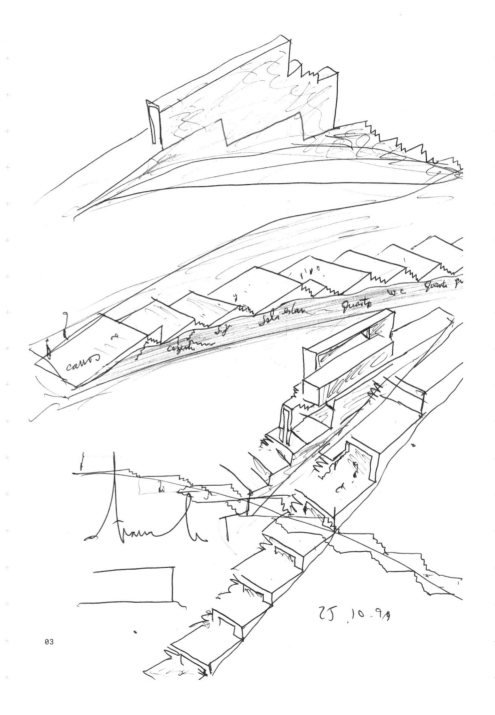

03

01
THE FINAL MODEL OF
CASA TÓLÓ

02
THE ARCHITECTURAL MODEL
SHOWS THE STEEPNESS OF
THE SITE

03
THE ARCHITECT'S
PRELIMINARY SKETCHES FOR
THE DIFFERENT LEVELS

05

06

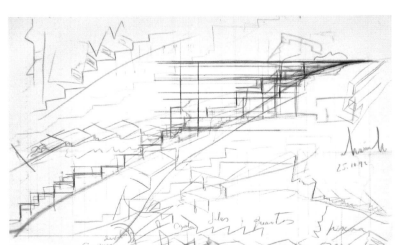

04

07

04
SOME OF THE ARCHITECT'S
STUDIES FOR CASA TÓLÓ

05
THE LIVING AREAS ARE
LIT BY NATURAL LIGHT
FROM ABOVE

06
THE HOUSE'S DIFFERENT
LEVELS ARE CONNECTED BY
A LONG INTERNAL STAIRCASE

07
ÁLVARO LEITE SIZA VIEIRA'S
VOLUME TESTS IN RELATION
TO THE SLOPE'S ANGLE

OPPOSITE
WITH ITS SQUARE SHAPE
AND PITCHED ROOF,
CASA EM AZEITÃO HAS
AN ALMOST CHILDLIKE
SIMPLICITY

RIGHT
THE GROUND-FLOOR LONG
FAÇADE OF THE HOUSE
OPENS UP ENTIRELY OR
CAN CLOSE COMPLETELY

Rural | CASA EM AZEITÃO
Atelier Central Arquitectos
Portugal

Almost resembling a child's drawing of a house, this is the home of a young family in Vila Nogueira de Azeitão, a small town south of Lisbon. With a plot located just above the bank of the river Tagus, the client's brief was for a structure with views towards the nearby Arrábida bridge, as well as the ability to close off the house against its immediate environment. Conceived by Lisbon-based Atelier Central Arquitectos, headed by Miguel Beleza, the house, completed in 2005, was designed not only to operate as a welcoming family home but also very much to resemble one from the outside.

Beleza played with archetypal residential forms, creating an almost stereotypically four-square structure with a pitched roof – the result of several building studies and tests of different roof designs and basic house shapes. For his choice of concrete forms the architect's references included La Congiunta museum in Switzerland, the work of the Swiss architect Peter Märkli. In a similar way, Beleza has employed plain geometrical forms, here combining them with basic colours to create bold but elemental compositions.

As Märkli did with La Congiunta, Beleza chose to use time as an ally, with the intention of creating a building that would age gracefully. Smooth and opaque at first sight, the concrete will age and change, and the process of staining and weathering was an integral part of the design from the very beginning. The extra layer created by time enhanced the structure's design and appearance; the inevitable, physical effects of oxidation and erosion, together with contrasting wet and dry concrete, were candidly incorporated into the aesthetic.

On the exterior, Beleza has used materials with inherent qualities of longevity and durability, designed to match his house design philosophy – raw naked concrete on the outside, covered with a zinc roof; Corten steel panels are used as blinds, protecting the deep-set glass windows.

Internally, the structure is organized across four levels. The basement hosts a garage and workshop, the ground floor the living and kitchen areas. On the first floor are the house's more private areas such as bedrooms, bathrooms and a study, while on the top floor the architect placed a joint music room and library. The interior design is equally simple, corresponding to the exterior, but softer, featuring mainly minimal white walls, timber and tiles.

Even though it adopts a slightly different approach, the interior makes a direct contribution to the form of the façades. The main circulation hub – the house's single, long staircase – spans across the entire north façade, and transitional semi-open spaces are created on the south and west sides through the wall's recesses. The house's harmoniously coordinated internal and external design embraces the client's requirements in a single residential shell.

Rural | CASA EM AZEITÃO
Atelier Central Arquitectos
Portugal

DIFFERENT VIEWS OF THE
HOUSE'S FINAL MODEL

04-05
CASA EM AZEITÃO'S
CONSTRUCTION; THE
CONCRETE HOUSE'S FINAL
VOLUME IS STARTING TO
TAKE SHAPE

01

02

04

05

07

03

08

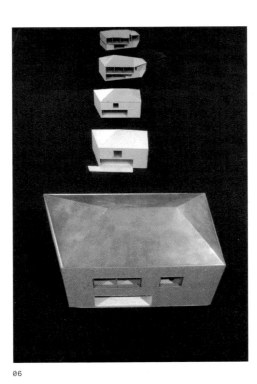

06

09

10

Rural | CASA NO GERÊS
Correia Ragazzi Arquitectos
Portugal

Located in Portugal's only protected nature reserve, the Peneda-Gerês National Park, the House in Gerês (Casa no Gerês, 2006) balances over a hillside in the Caniçada area of Vieira do Minho, in the mountains north of Porto, towards the Spanish border.

The project began in 2003, when the clients, Micé and Eduardo Pinto Ferreira, discovered a small, beautiful plot of land of just over 4000 square metres (43,000 square feet) in the national park, on the edge of the Cávado River. Keen water-skiers, they decided that it was the ideal location for their weekend retreat. They called on Porto-based architects Graça Correia and Roberto Ragazzi for the commission and three years later, the final touches were being added to the striking 150 square metre (1600 square foot) Casa no Gerês.

The architects' inspiration was drawn from various construction solutions for long, cantilevered structures, such as the Casa Malaparte in Italy by Adalberto Libera, as well as from product design, for example Jean Nouvel's 'Less' table. For this commission, the brief outlined a house for the couple and their only child, along with a separate guest room that could double as a storehouse for water-skiing equipment. This space would also contain a shower, bathroom and storage area. Additionally, given the protected surroundings, the structure had to have a strong presence but also work in harmony with nature. According to the architects, 'the house could only exist if it was a significant element in the landscape'.

Certain specific conditions had to be met, as dictated by the protected area's regulations. For example, the building had to be of concrete construction and all the existing trees should remain untouched. An old ruin located on the site had to be preserved and incorporated into the solution, adding to the project's particular and delicate nature. The ruin was small and defined the whole scale of the intervention, since the area of the house had to be adjusted accordingly. The structure's placement within the plot, equally, was crucial.

The best solution, offering the necessary space for the house to breathe and also meeting the obligatory protection standards for the landscape, was achieved by a long cantilevered structure, which juts for almost one third of the house's total length above the steep slope and overlooking the riverbank. The overhanging part appears almost weightless, while the big openings and floor-to-ceiling glass used in the side façades make the whole building look even lighter and more transparent.

In order to deal with the project's special engineering needs, the architects collaborated with structural, hydraulic and foundation engineers GOP. The building is half-buried to balance the hanging weight, while the flat roof is accessible and transforms into a pleasant open summer terrace. The interior is entirely clad with birch.

Combining the concrete's plasticity and sculptural effect against the abundant flora with the functional requirements of the challenging site, architects Correia Ragazzi delivered a functional solution that manages to be visually dramatic at the same time as minimizing the building's effect on its natural surroundings.

Rural | CASA NO GERÊS
Correia Ragazzi Arquitectos
Portugal

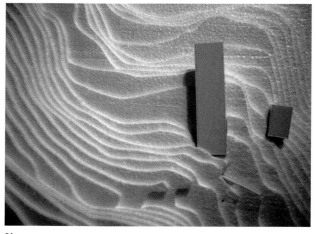

01

02

<u>01</u>
THE HOUSE'S MODEL SHOT
FROM ABOVE, SHOWING
THE HOUSE IN RELATION
TO ITS SURROUNDINGS

<u>02</u>
THE FINAL MODEL
OF CASA NO GERÊS

<u>03</u>
THE ARCHITECTS'
STUDIES FOR THE
HOUSE'S FRONT FAÇADE

03

04

05

<u>04</u>
COLOURED SKETCH OF A
SIDE VIEW OF THE HOUSE

<u>05</u>
COLOURED SKETCH OF
THE HOUSE AS SEEN FROM
THE TOP OF THE HILL

<u>06</u>
SIDE VIEW SHOWING CASA
NO GERÊS'S PROJECTING
FORM, IN CONTRAST TO
THE SLOPE

06

Rural | **LA RUINA HABITADA**
Jesús Castillo Oli
Spain

The conversion is inevitably an architectural hybrid and all too often the site of a furious struggle between styles and approaches, as the new attempts to make an indelible mark on the old. It goes without saying that a successful conversion is perhaps the most pragmatic, sensible and sustainable architecture of all, creatively reusing and improving without recourse to extensive new materials. Yet the successful conversion is not architecture entirely without ego.

La Ruina Habitada (2006) was created by the Spanish architect Jesús Castillo Oli, a restoration expert with extensive experience of working within ruined structures. This domestic conversion presented a very different challenge. Located in Porquera de los Infantes, a small village in Spain's northern province of Palencia, the raw material was the shell of an abandoned house, stripped back to striated walls of brick and flint, with gaping windows and the sorry remnants of a roof. The local environment is a relatively impoverished post-agricultural community.

The client, Fernando Gallo, is hotel editor for Spain's *El Pais* newspaper. Gallo briefed Oli to create a 'rural loft' – a house that could function both as an entertainment space and as a private retreat without spoiling the earthy, industrial qualities of the original ruin. The rawness of the finishes has been mitigated by seamless contemporary insertions, including frameless and mullion-less windows that fill the voids in the brick fabric while also recalling their vacant state. One half of the structure has been left open to the elements, with a meticulously raked Zen garden, installed by landscape specialist Ricardo Zendrera, at ground level.

The inhabited ruin covers a total area of 115 square metres (1240 square feet), with a series of glass, iron, steel and wood structures slotted into the shell. Key architectural elements include the Japanese-style covered courtyard, or *engawa*, plus a large wine cellar and an enormous walk-in shower. The 'empty' windows now form frames for the distant mountain views, and the restored original timbers and brick are laid bare by the extensive use of glass. Gallo and Oli have attempted to bring warmth and human scale to the structure.

Although there is a system of computer-controlled lighting at the heart of the house, including colour-shifting LEDs, the experience of the house is dictated by the movement of the sun. With no blinds or curtains, the direct sunlight creates bold shadows that redefine the double-height interior throughout the day. The pared-down detailing is highly specific to the client's requirements. With its underfloor heating and no proper kitchen, La Ruina Habitada offers a very singular take on the reconstruction and reuse of old buildings, eschewing gloss and newness in favour of memory and patina as the integral components of the home.

01

01
THE EXISTING WINDOWS
ARE PARTLY REUSED,
PARTLY LEFT BLANK

02
INSIDE, THE HOUSE IS
BISECTED BY A GLAZED WALL

03
FRAMELESS GLASS
MAXIMIZES THE OPENINGS
ON TO THE LANDSCAPE

02

03

04

05

06

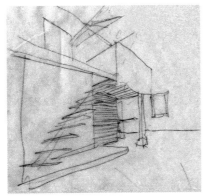

07

04–05
THE EXISTING RUIN
BEFORE THE CONVERSION

06–07
INITIAL DESIGN
SKETCHES, SHOWING THE
GLASS WALL AND SKELETAL
STAIRCASE CONCEPT

THIS PAGE
CASA EN EL CAMPO IS
THE SUBSTANTIAL
RECONSTRUCTION OF AN
EXISTING SHELTER

OPPOSITE
THE DRY-STONE WALL
IS MATCHED WITH A
CONTEMPORARY METAL
SLIDING FAÇADE

Rural | CASA EN EL CAMPO
Juan Herreros Arquitectos
Spain

Juan Herreros's Casa en el Campo (2007) in Mallorca is actually a conversion of an existing structure, an old refuge for shepherds set on a plain amid rocky outcrops. The original building had a mono-pitched roof, and Herreros's studio simply 'doubled' the volume, mirroring it symmetrically in order to create an inverted roof with a central valley gutter. The kitchen, bedroom and bathroom are located to the north of the plan, while to the south are the dining room, living room and study. In this way, the allocation of space mimics the original 'primitive compartments' that related directly to the original functions of the building, in which different spaces were given over to living, keeping animals and storing animal feed.

The Casa en el Campo is markedly more sophisticated in its detailing than the original structure. The dry-stone outer walling has been restored, enhanced and extended. The centre valley of the new roof serves to collect precious rainwater, which is stored for reuse within the house. Natural ventilation is facilitated by the house's orientation, allowing the wind to cool the interior by means of a series of fully openable upper and lower windows and a series of sliding shutters and folding window lights that open or close to provide differing levels of shade or light, creating a changeable and highly practical façade.

The emphasis on minimal detailing that evokes the structure's original use is carried through in the interior furnishings. The corrugated metal shutters are painted an industrial green, lighter and more distinct than the surrounding vegetation but not in any way dominant. When empty, the shutters can be closed completely, leaving the house as an abstract, abandoned object in the landscape.

Rural | CASA EN EL CAMPO
Juan Herreros Arquitectos
Spain

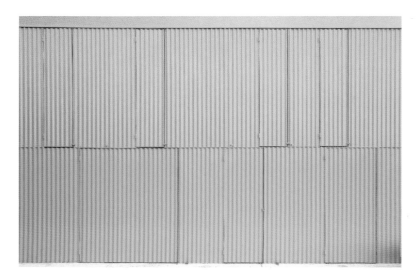

01

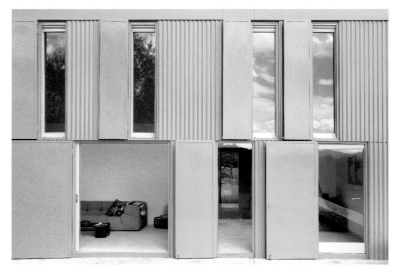

02

03

<u>01</u>
THE METAL SHUTTERS ARE
SET AT HIGH AND LOW LEVEL
IN THE DOUBLE-HEIGHT
LIVING AREA

<u>02</u>
SHUTTERS OPENED,
LIVING AREA

<u>03</u>
THE HOUSE AT DUSK

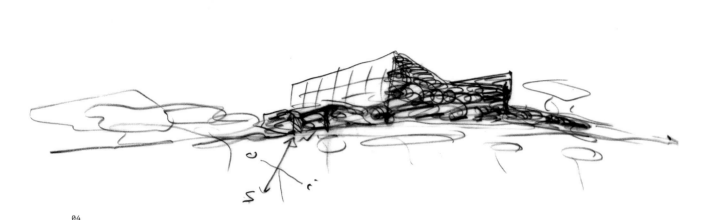

04

04
INITIAL DESIGN
SKETCH ILLUSTRATING
THE VALLEY ROOF

05
THE MAIN LIVING AREA

06
SOUTH AND NORTH FAÇADES;
THE HOUSE IS SET
INTO A SLOPING SITE

05

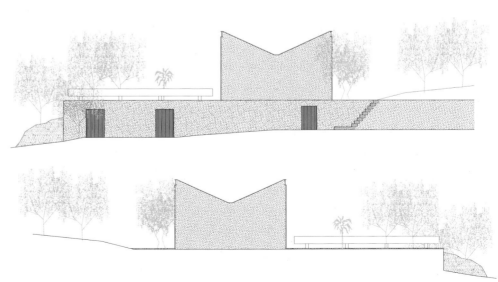

06

Rural | GRIMETON NATURE RESERVE BUILDING
Strata Arkitektur
Sweden

Designed by the Stockholm-based studio Strata Arkitektur and overseen by Petra Gipp and Katarina Lundeberg, the Grimeton Nature Reserve building (2007) serves as a refuge – a place of retreat and relaxation for the forestry guards who work in the reserve. Grimeton, in southern Sweden, is home to the 1924 Varberg radio transmitter, still in working condition and a World Heritage Site since 2004. The landscape is dominated by beech forests, which extend over an area of 50 square kilometres (19 square miles).

The new refuge was built on a ridge above Lake Rörsjön, the junction between the old forest and the managed landscape of modern forestry. Further down the slope is a barn, also designed by Strata. The refuge is raised up off the forest floor on concrete piloti. With three walls clad in tarred wood and one wall of glass – overlooking the lake to the south-west – the building forms a simple, abstract composition, arranged in two stepped volumes, one back, one forward. The façade is dark and textured, while simple detailing such as the folded-steel staircases speak of a building dedicated to function, in this case sheltering those who 'care and administer the forest for forthcoming generations'.

Inside, the L-shaped plan pushes all services to the outer walls, including a bathroom, two small bunk rooms, a master bedroom and galley kitchen. This leaves a generous living area, the tall windows framing an evocative view over the forest and lake. The concrete chimney-breast is set off by wooden floors and walls, teak-framed windows and metal steps. Hard-wearing areas such as the bathroom and kitchen are floored in concrete. The house is designed so that the solid, sculptural fireplace is the element that would endure the longest, perhaps allowing another structure to be erected around it on the same site in the distant future.

The architects were well aware of the responsibility of building within a nature reserve. The resulting house is understated and modest, its only concession to drama being the magnificent – and highly appropriate – views.

THIS PAGE
FINISHES AND FORMS
ARE A DELIBERATE
ATTEMPT TO 'DEFY
POLISHED SUPERFLUITY'

OPPOSITE
MATERIALS ARE LEFT RAW
AND UNTREATED, WITH
FULL-HEIGHT DOORS,
ROOFLIGHTS AND DOUBLE-
HEIGHT SPACES CREATING
INTRIGUE AND DRAMA

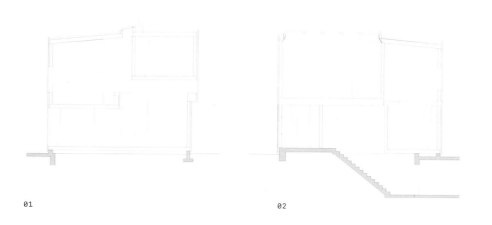

01

02

03

04

01-03
SECTIONAL VIEWS: THE
HOUSE INCORPORATES TWO
ARTIST'S STUDIOS WITH
A NUMBER OF LEVELS

04
PRESENTATION MODEL OF THE
GROUND FLOOR, DOMINATED
BY THE STUDIO SPACE

05
THE NEW HOUSE IS SITED ON
A PLOT ADJACENT TO THE
CLIENT'S FORMER RESIDENCE

05

06

06
WORKING MODEL. THE HOUSE
IS A COMPLEX ARRANGEMENT
OF SPACE, UNITED BY THE
STAIRCASE ON THE AXIS OF
THE L-SHAPED PLAN

07-08
LIGHT STUDIES TAKEN FROM
A PRESENTATION MODEL

07

08

SET HARD AGAINST
THE SLOPES, EM2N
ARCHITEKTEN'S MOUNTAIN
CHALET IS A MONOLITHIC
BLACK PRESENCE AGAINST
THE SNOW. THE WOOD-
CLAD STRUCTURE FEATURES
HIGH-LEVEL LIVING
AREAS AND EXPANSIVE
VIEWS ACROSS THE VALLEY

il MOUNTAIN CHALET
EM2N Architekten
Switzerland

Set high in the Swiss Alps, this holiday cottage (2003) is arranged like a miniature fortress, with stacked accommodation and an angular façade to protect it against avalanches. Dubbed a 'tower chalet' by its designers, Zürich-based EM2N Architekten (Mathias Müller and Daniel Niggli), the form was arrived at by the desire to bring views to the chalet, traditionally a low-lying structure. The architects describe the majority of holiday houses as being 'like conventional single-family houses … they might as well be houses from ready-made house catalogues, their architectural expression is accordingly arbitrary'.

Determined to make the most of the steep site, the architects built upward, not along. Right alongside the chalet is a ski slope (a meadow during the summer), and a cable-car hums along close to the upper floors. By raising the house up high – the living spaces are on the upper floor – 360-degree views of the Alpine landscape have been achieved. The decision was made to leave the plot unmarked, so no fences break up the ground between house and ski run, leaving it like a monolithic insertion into the mountainside. The upper storeys are demarcated by the large frameless windows, with smaller, shuttered windows on the lower levels, while dark-stained wood cladding makes a clear reference to traditional mountain architecture.

The plan was arranged to exploit the qualities of holiday living rather than conventional day-to-day life. 'Where does the difference between everyday and holiday living lie?' the architects ask, demonstrating their answer through the utterly stripped-back floor plan, which effectively gives over a single function to each floor level, united by a circular spiral staircase. This industrial unit is sheathed in a tube of semi-transparent mesh, part of a materials palette that is raw and uncompromising, placing the emphasis on the luxury of space rather than on finishes or expensive items.

From the concrete basement, which contains storage space, a WC and a boiler room, the stair leads up to a sleeping area, secluded and dark thanks to its small windows. A circular bath and shower forms a sculptural counterpoint to the stair, and is sheathed in the same semi-transparent mesh; a similar device is utilized again on the top floor, where a suspended fireplace sits above a circular hearth. The interior dimensions of the building are modest – 104 square metres (1120 square feet) of habitable space – and the cost of the project compared favourably to a conventional chalet.

Inside, the walls, floors and ceilings are finished in OSB (oriented strand board), a low-cost building material usually covered with a final finish. Rather than disguise the material, the architects have relished the rough visual texture created by the compression of thousands of strips of thin timber, so that the interiors have a unique atmosphere. Services such as electrics and plumbing are affixed simply to the wooden walls, the exposed features creating an honest and purposeful space. 'The luxury of the house is not manifested in expensive detailing and materials, but in its location and spaces.'

LEFT
THE FIRST-FLOOR BEDROOM
AND BATHROOM AREA
IS A QUIET HAVEN
LINED IN OSB WITH
A SHEATHED INDUSTRIAL
SPIRAL STAIRCASE CUTTING
THROUGH THE SPACE

RIGHT
THE TOP-FLOOR LIVING AREA
FEATURES GENEROUS
FLOOR-TO-CEILING GLAZING
AND INDUSTRIAL FINISHES

01

<u>01</u>
THE BASEMENT, WITH ITS
WALLS OF PREFABRICATED,
PATTERNED CONCRETE
PANELS, IS ATMOSPHERIC
AND MYSTERIOUS

<u>02-03</u>
DETAILS OF THE STUDDED
CONCRETE PANELS,
FABRICATED IN ADVANCE
AND USED TO FORM THE
BASEMENT WALLS

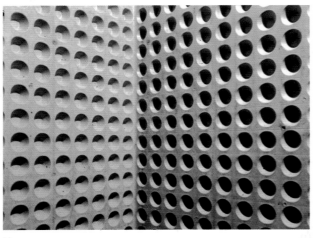

02

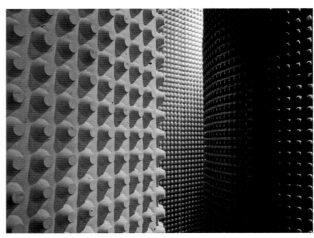

03

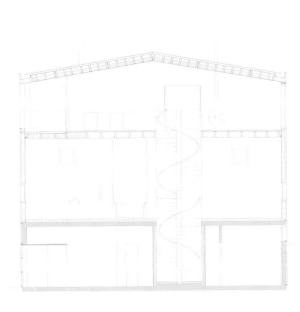

04

05

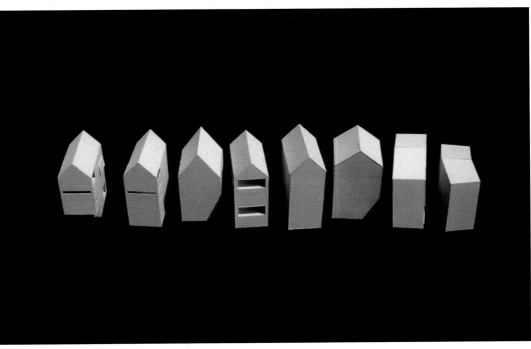

04
SECTION THROUGH THE
CHALET, SHOWING THE DARK
BASEMENT, THE MODEST
WINDOWS IN THE SLEEPING
SPACE AND THE HIGHLY
GLAZED TOP FLOOR

05
VIEWED FROM DOWN THE
SLOPE, EM2N'S DESIGN
IS SEEN IN THE CONTEXT
OF TRADITIONAL ALPINE
ARCHITECTURE

06
MASSING MODELS, EXPLORING
THE EVOLUTION OF THE
HOUSE'S FINAL FORM

06

RIGHT
THE GARDEN FAÇADE
IS AUSTERE AND
UNCOMPROMISING, WITH
ONLY THE POOL HINTING
AT DOMESTIC OCCUPATION

LEFT
SET AT THE BASE OF THE
SITE, THE GARAGE IS
ILLUMINATED BY A SINGLE
SHAFT OF LIGHT FROM
ABOVE; THE CONCRETE
BUTTRESS SUPPORTS THE
SWIMMING POOL

Rural | HOUSE IN BRIONE
Wespi de Meuron Architekten
Switzerland

Jérôme de Meuron and Markus Wespi built this stone and concrete house for a client in the canton of Ticino, Switzerland, in 2004–5. The surrounding area is upmarket but undistinctive, featuring large detached villas scattered across the hillside, overlooking Locarno and Lake Maggiore. With a floor area of 155 square metres (1670 square feet), the new house is startlingly different from its ersatz, pseudo-Mediterranean neighbours, presenting a deliberately austere and almost faceless image to the world.

The architects conceived the house as an antidote to the 'chaos of the urban sprawl'. As a result, they deliberately avoided the 'conventional attributes of

a classical house'. Instead, the new property is conceived of as 'two simple cubes emerging from the hill', a piece of sculptural landscape art rather than a building. Nestled into the site, the house contains a living area and kitchen on the ground floor, along with a pool jutting out above the steep site. On the floor above, the sleeping quarters are given a cell-like insularity, a floating 'box' with views on to two internal courtyards only.

Perhaps most dramatic of all is the cave-like garage. This is entered at the base of the site and is linked to the house by means of a staircase, which ascends beneath the pool. The space is lit by a single-slot rooflight, which sends a shifting shaft of daylight

across both the stone walls and the concrete swimming pool structure.

The house is far removed from the late Modernist archetype of the glassy box, having just two large openings in the stone wall structure, each covered with a movable wooden grid that doubles as a security gate. Instead of walls of glass, a series of slots and internal courts brings in light without compromising privacy. Internal finishes mirror the exterior surfaces – stone floors and walls with exposed concrete lintels and floor slabs subdivided by walls of frameless glass.

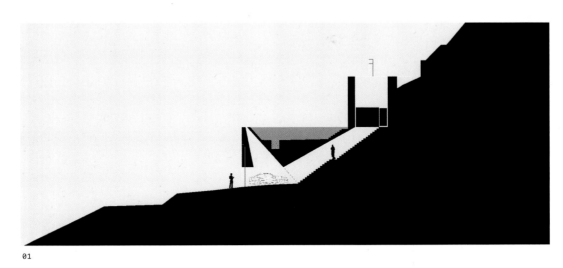

01

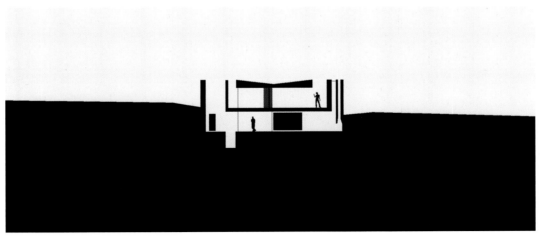

02

THE HOUSE OVERLOOKS LAKE
MAGGIORE. LIGHT WELLS
– SEEN HERE – BRING
DAYLIGHT INTO THE
CLOISTERED INTERIOR

01–02
SITE SECTIONS,
ILLUSTRATING THE DEEP
BASEMENT AND GARAGE
BENEATH THE POOL,
AND THE SUSPENDED
FIRST-FLOOR 'TRAY'

Rural | BUTTERWELL FARMHOUSE
Charles Barclay Architects
UK

Building within the rural landscape is one of the flashpoints of debate regarding architectural form, appropriateness and context. Legislation designed to preserve a local vernacular or stylistic form exists in numerous countries, from regional codes up to national policy. The debate is muddied by the comparative lack of regulations surrounding agricultural buildings, which are frequently off-the-shelf structures designed without architectural involvement.

In many parts of Britain there is a great paucity of affordable rural housing. Could the ad hoc agricultural approach be translated into housing provision? Charles Barclay Architects was commissioned to create a farmhouse for a Cornish dairy farmer. Located in the Looe Valley in the south of the county, it is built of timber, low-cost, sustainable and energy-efficient. Cut into a south-facing hillside, Butterwell Farmhouse (2004) places an open-plan living space on the first floor and bedrooms below, with two bridges providing level access from the hillside above. High levels of insulation keep running costs to a minimum.

The 167 square metre (1800 square foot) structure was highly economical to build.

The combination of weather-boarded walls and traditional slate roof gives the house a straightforward, stark appearance, deliberately contrasting with the landscape. Barclay writes that the farmhouse 'was intended to have the ad hoc quality of a temporary installation and inspiration was drawn from the kit houses of the 19th-century pioneer farmers in the American Midwest, often purchased from catalogues and put up by the newly arrived farmer and his neighbours'. The farmhouse is effectively a modern archetype, a demonstration of how prefabrication methods (used here for the timber frame) can be employed to convey a sense of domestic scale, a 'homestead in the landscape'. Keeping the interior as simple and basic as the exterior shape, while referencing the 'practical needs of the working farmer', the architect used abstraction and pragmatism to create a contemporary version of the traditional farmhouse.

THIS PAGE
THE FARMHOUSE WALLS ARE
WEATHER-BOARDED AND
UNADORNED. THE HOUSE IS
SET INTO A SLOPE,
ACCESSED VIA A BRIDGE AT
FIRST-FLOOR LEVEL

OPPOSITE, LEFT
THE CORNISH LANDSCAPE IS
DOTTED WITH AD HOC
TIN-ROOFED HOMES AND
AGRICULTURAL STRUCTURES

OPPOSITE, RIGHT
AXONOMETRIC VIEW OF
BUTTERWELL FARMHOUSE

THE NEW ADDITION, SEEN
ALONGSIDE THE EXISTING
19TH-CENTURY CHAPEL.
BLACKENED TIMBER CLADDING
REFERENCES THE ORIGINAL
TIN TABERNACLES
OF SOUTHERN ENGLAND

Rural | PROVIDENCE CHAPEL
Jonathan Tuckey Design
UK

The London-based architect Jonathan Tuckey specializes in reuse and restoration, eschewing the glory of the all-new structure in favour of a combination of retained patina, structural expressiveness and added function. Following on from the architect's own residence, the Collage House in North London (2006), Tuckey's studio completed the Providence Chapel in 2009. Located in the Wiltshire village of Colerne, this modest but dignified Baptist chapel was built in 1867 and used continuously until its eventual sale in 2004.

The chapel represented a typically organic structure, slowly added to throughout its life, expanding the original fabric of the building as demands for such facilities as storage and toilets were gradually added to the list of required functions. While the Bath stone chapel resembled a miniature temple set within its own walled garden, the additional accretions were less solid, save for a small schoolroom to the rear. Ultimately they restricted access to the rear garden and were not in keeping with the proportions or materials of the chapel.

In order successfully to convert the building into a practical living space, Tuckey removed the additions and replaced them with a new-build structure. This new, subsidiary space allowed the tall original space of the chapel to be retained as a living room and kitchen area, leading through to a study. A glazed link provides access to the new structure, which contains bedroom accommodation for the clients and their children, along with roof-lit bathrooms and a utility area.

Tuckey describes the extension as 'complementing, not competing with, the scale and status of the chapel itself'. The use of blackened timber cladding makes the new structure a shadow cast by the original building, with its warm stone walls and slate roof. The new material evokes the so-called 'tin tabernacles' developed in the first half of the 19th century, as new corrugation and galvanization processes enabled sheet steel to be used as a durable, weather-tight and cost-effective cladding. Tin tabernacles, characteristic of this area, were necessarily simple, unadorned, pitched-roof buildings with a quasi-industrial appearance.

The Providence Chapel extension is an example of the benefits of careful reuse and reintegration, demonstrating that new elements can exist alongside the old without pastiche or imitation. While the careful choice of materials hints at the history of the site, the massing of the new extension sets up an architectural rhythm, with the three irregular roof pitches stepping up the shallow slope of the site. Additional benefits include greatly improved environmental performance, thanks to better insulation and the use of recycled and low-impact materials.

The unity between old and new is continued throughout the project, with original elements such as floors, pews and the timber gallery all restored and contrasted with new-build elements such as the dining table, kitchen island unit and totemic bookcase, located on the site of the pulpit. In the extension, finishes are modest and sparse – concrete floors, unpainted plaster walls and joinery made from fibreboard. The economic expediency of the fit-out recalls the simplicity of the original chapel interior, which dated from a period of religious austerity.

Tuckey taught at the University of Greenwich alongside the architect and educator Fred Scott, the author of *On Altering Architecture*[1] (see p. 17). The strong sense of continuity and pragmatism demonstrated in this project is entirely sympathetic to Scott's point of view: 'A building must not be changed beyond recognition, its essential nature has to be assured by the work of alteration, discerned by the act of alteration; its poetic nature depends on it.'

1 | Fred Scott, <u>On Altering Architecture</u>, Routledge, London, 2008

01

02

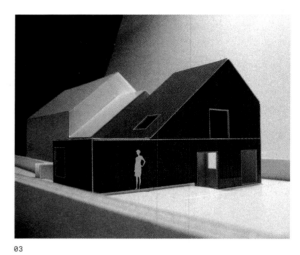

03

04

05

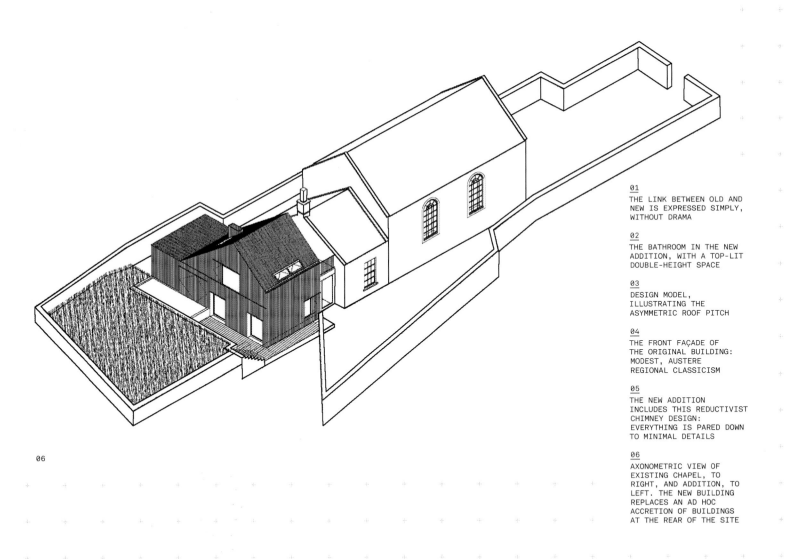

01
THE LINK BETWEEN OLD AND
NEW IS EXPRESSED SIMPLY,
WITHOUT DRAMA

02
THE BATHROOM IN THE NEW
ADDITION, WITH A TOP-LIT
DOUBLE-HEIGHT SPACE

03
DESIGN MODEL,
ILLUSTRATING THE
ASYMMETRIC ROOF PITCH

04
THE FRONT FAÇADE OF
THE ORIGINAL BUILDING:
MODEST, AUSTERE
REGIONAL CLASSICISM

05
THE NEW ADDITION
INCLUDES THIS REDUCTIVIST
CHIMNEY DESIGN:
EVERYTHING IS PARED DOWN
TO MINIMAL DETAILS

06
AXONOMETRIC VIEW OF
EXISTING CHAPEL, TO
RIGHT, AND ADDITION, TO
LEFT. THE NEW BUILDING
REPLACES AN AD HOC
ACCRETION OF BUILDINGS
AT THE REAR OF THE SITE

06

ON A REMOTE SITE IN
COLORADO, INSTEAD OF AN
ERSATZ LOG-CABIN, THE
ARCHITECT CREATED A
MODERN PAVILION USING
SIMPLE BUILDING MATERIALS

Rural | WILLIAMS CABIN
Stephen Atkinson Architecture
USA

The Williams Cabin (2007) is a compact rural single-room studio, vaguely anthropomorphic in form (thanks to the twin bay, door and shutter arrangement that gives the house a discernible 'face') and a therefore friendly addition to a piece of remote high ground on the edge of a forest in Colorado. The interior of the tiny cabin, 7.3 metres square (24 feet square) is heated by a single cast-iron stove, and is paired with a covered deck measuring exactly the same floor area as the room (26.75 square metres [288 square feet]). The bath and toilet are pushed to one edge of the plan, hidden behind a compact kitchen unit.

Atkinson is unafraid to engage with the vernacular as well as the relatively untested arena of modular house construction. His prefabricated Zachary House project was constructed for display in the Mall of America before being auctioned off for charity. 'This meant that the final location in the US, climate, site, etc, couldn't be known early on,' Atkinson says. 'So in some ways a generic American "house" and site was the only appropriate way to approach the problem.'

In Colorado, the brief was not for a permanent home but rather for a vacation cabin, a place to sleep, cook and bathe, using an aesthetic that was not an overfamiliar cliché. As Atkinson puts it, 'the request from the client for his site was for a cabin that would be sustainable, fire-resistant, and not be a log cabin'. On a site high above sea level, looking west across a river

valley, the project was off the grid and intended to be as low-impact as possible.

The building itself is set atop a recessed base, making it appear to float in the environment. All materials – predominantly wood framing and plywood infill – were sourced from sustainably harvested forests. Paints were non-toxic, the exterior plaster was lime-based and the wall finishes in the bathroom areas were mud plaster. The kitchen counter is concrete, fabricated by a local company using a specially developed eco-cement called Lithistone, with '1/20th of the embodied energy of concrete'. In addition, the wood used in the fit-out and for the furniture was sourced from dead trees around the large site or from trees that had to be felled during the construction of the access road. The main space has lino flooring and panelling made from locally grown aspen wood, while the interior doors are made using eco-resin and the 'insulation is from soy-based spray urethane and shredded/recycled denim'. Protection from forest fires is greatly improved by the plaster stucco exterior finish, metal roof and special fire shutters.

Atkinson's earlier projects, such as the Hudson Residence in Maryland, draw extensively on vernacular forms, forming picturesque groupings rather than monolithic structures. Because of its scale and location the Williams Cabin is a more contemporary statement, the reduction of living space down to the bare essentials.

Rural | WILLIAMS CABIN
Stephen Atkinson Architecture
USA

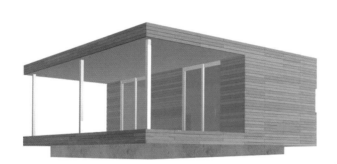

01

02

03

04

01
COMPUTER MODEL OF
THE CONSTRUCTION: THE
COVERED PORCH OCCUPIES
THE SAME FLOOR AREA AS
THE CABIN ITSELF

02
UNDER CONSTRUCTION:
THE WALLS ARE HEAVILY
INSULATED AGAINST
THE COLORADAN WINTER

03
THE CABIN IS RAISED
UP ON A STEEL FRAME
TO PRESERVE THE SITE

04
THE REAR FAÇADE UNDER
CONSTRUCTION. STANDARD
WOODEN PANELS FACILITATED
THE BUILD

05

Rural | C-I HOUSE
Paul Cha Architect
USA

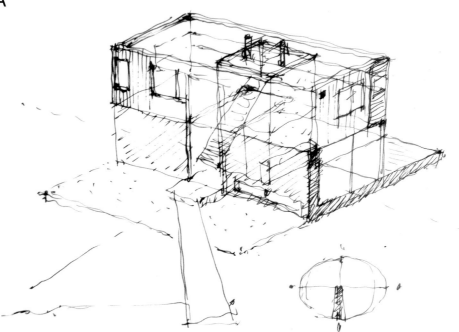

This country retreat is located on a generous 1.6 hectare (4 acre) site in Hudson Valley, just two hours from New York City. Paul Cha's design for the C-I House (2007) was inspired by a vernacular archetype, the New England saltbox, a form of wooden-framed and clapboard-clad architecture developed during America's colonial era. Simple, adaptable and expedient, the typical saltbox house featured a long stretch of pitched roof that sloped down from a two-storey front façade to a single storey at the rear, in this way avoiding the taxation levied on a two-storey building.

The C-I House consists of 185 square metres (2000 square feet) of accommodation, an expansive rectangular box constructed to precise dimensions: 15 metres long by 6 metres wide by 7.6 metres high (50 x 20 x 25 feet), with a 3.3 metre (11 foot) ground floor and a 2.7 metre (9 foot) first floor. It is constructed from a combination of poured concrete (the slab and rear wall) and structural timber framing and infill. The concrete was required by local building regulations, while the extensive use of wood allowed the architect to utilize standard modular construction dimensions, saving time and money.

The house is set in the centre of the plot, reached by an access road that swings around to meet the east façade. An elevated ramp leads up to the front door, which is treated like a slot set into the concrete slab, which 'folds' up through 90 degrees to create the façade. The ground floor is arranged as an open-plan space around a service core, which contains the WC, storage, utility and kitchen areas. The west façade is extensively glazed, opening out on to a sun deck with views back across the site. The first floor is a more private space, partitioned into two bedrooms – master and guest – a bathroom and study.

Cha describes the project as a 'modern reinterpretation of the house on the prairie', and the entire project is constructed to a very human scale, celebrating the craft processes involved in the construction, rather than abstracting them. Drawing inspiration from projects as diverse as Le Corbusier's Villa Garches, the architecture of Gordon Matta-Clark and Marcello Gandini's car designs for Bertone, the C-I House has a strong relationship with the land, a composition of solids and voids that retains an emotional resonance.

THIS PAGE
THE C-I HOUSE STRIPS
DOMESTIC DESIGN BACK TO A
BARE MINIMUM. WINDOW
FRAMES STAND PROUD OF THE
CONCRETE AND WOOD FAÇADE

OPPOSITE
ORIGINAL DESIGN SKETCH OF
THE C-I HOUSE, WITH THE
THICK 'FOLDED' CONCRETE
SLAB FORMING THE GROUND
FLOOR AND WALL

Rural | C-I HOUSE
Paul Cha Architect
USA

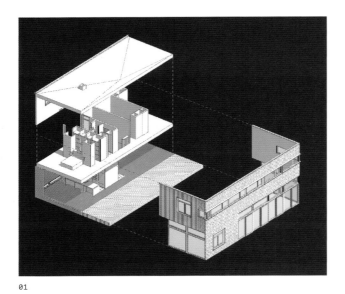

01

01
EXPLODED AXONOMETRIC
DRAWING ILLUSTRATING
CONSTRUCTION ELEMENTS

02
A AN ELEVATED RAMP CUTS
   THROUGH THE MANICURED
   GARDEN
B FOUNDATION SLAB
   FOLDING UP VERTICALLY
C A SQUARE SERVICE CORE
D LIVING ROOM AND
   DINING ROOM
E METAL-FRAMED GLASS
   PLANES
F SUN DECK
G A TWO-STOREY ATRIUM
   WITH A STAIRCASE
H THE SECOND FLOOR'S
   SERVICE CORE
I BEDROOM HALL
J HORIZONTAL STRIP
   WINDOW
K SQUARE AND
   RECTANGULAR WINDOWS
L DIFFERENT TEXTURES
   THAT DISINTEGRATE THE
   SALT BOX TYPOLOGY

02

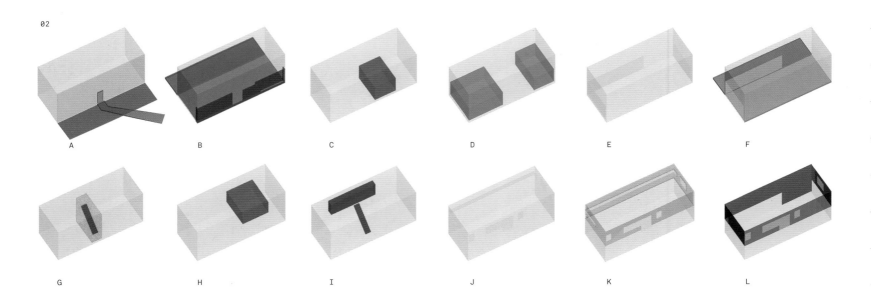

A B C D E F

G H I J K L

03

04

05

03–05
THE HOUSE UNDER
CONSTRUCTION, THE POURED
SLAB SUPPORTING THE
WOODEN FRAME

06
PAUL CHA'S WATERCOLOUR
SKETCHES OF THE HOUSE
BREAK EACH COMPONENT DOWN
INTO A COLOURED ELEMENT,
EMPHASIZING THE ABSTRACT
COMPOSITION

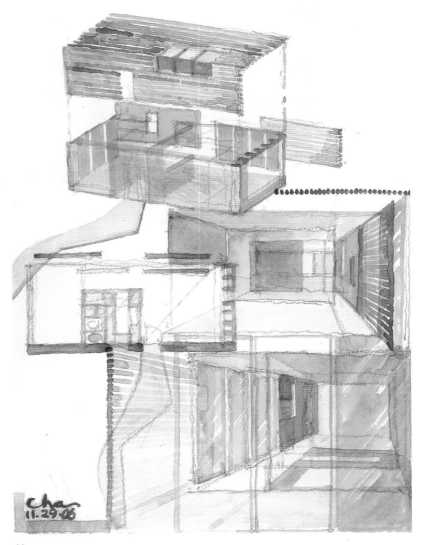

06

Suburban

Suburban | PA1 HOUSE IN ZURNDORF
Popelka Poduschka Architekten (PPAG)
Austria

The directors of young Austrian practice PPAG, Anna Popelka and Georg Poduschka, believe firmly that architecture is far more of a science than an art. By committing themselves to adopting a different approach for each project, the PPAG portfolio is varied and eclectic.

A typical example of their unique and science-oriented approach is the PA1 single-family house, built in 2005 in the village of Zurndorf, about 60 kilometres (37 miles) away from their Vienna studio. The project's challenges were clear from the very beginning; the plot was in an old apple orchard, and one of the client's requests was to leave every single tree intact. The architects also had to work within a modest budget.

In order to develop the best solution, they used the practice's experience in temporary installation design, where there is more leeway for experimentation in both materials and design. The team researched the house in a similar way to an impermanent building to find both materials and building methods that would suit the site and the budget.

The outcome was the element that immediately comes across as the most striking and unusual aspect of the house: its trademark skin texture. The building's grey, rough-looking exterior quality inspired the architects to nickname it jokingly 'elephant skin house', but a scientific explanation underlies their choice. The house's external shell includes a layer of strand boards, sprayed with polyurethane foam coating and a UV-protective layer, which covers the small building entirely.

Popelka and Poduschka discovered the particular material – a special foam – in a completely different context, when they were part of a team designing a Climate Wind Tunnel. The material, which in that project was used to coat large tubes for energy-saving purposes, was later employed by the architects in the design of a series of yard furniture. Because of its energy-saving insulation qualities and flexibility, they soon decided to test it for architectural design and PA1.

The house's interiors are slightly more conventional, clad almost entirely with plywood panels, with an exposed timber beam ceiling. The house's comfortable yet straightforward orthogonal layout comprises two bedrooms, a bathroom and an open-plan living/kitchen/dining area, and features double-height spaces and big windows towards the orchard.

PPAG had to develop their design in a very short time, and even though they were still not 100 per cent confident with handling the unorthodox material, they cleverly managed to apply it on the house's different elements, even including the roof, for which they needed an altogether separate study.

Successfully incorporated in the house's design, not only did the unusual padding technique easily enable the building to meet the local insulation requirements, it also helped the architects to fulfil the clients' needs in a very simple, energy-efficient and cost-effective way.

THIS PAGE
PA1 WAS ORIENTATED
SO THAT ITS LARGE
OPENINGS OFFER SWEEPING
VIEWS TOWARDS THE OLD
APPLE ORCHARD

OPPOSITE
PA1'S SKIN, WITH
ITS TRADEMARK ROUGH
TEXTURE, IS MADE OF
POLYURETHANE FOAM

Suburban | PA1 HOUSE IN ZURNDORF
Popelka Poduschka Architekten (PPAG)
Austria

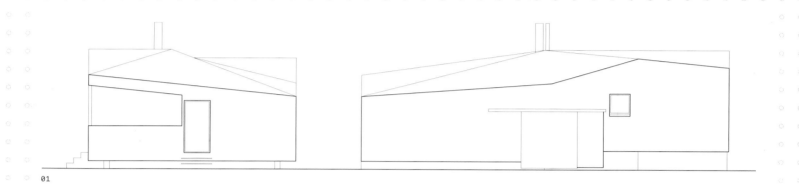

01

01
THE HOUSE'S
SIMPLE FRONT
AND SIDE FAÇADES

02-04
DIFFERENT VIEWS OF
PA1'S WORKING MODEL

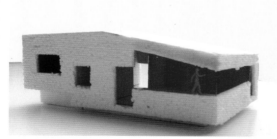

02

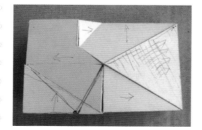

03

04

05

08

09

06

07

05

THE HOUSE'S WARM WOODEN
INTERIOR IS SIMPLE AND
THE ROOF WAS ESPECIALLY
DESIGNED TO FOLD OVER
THE STRUCTURE'S
IRREGULAR SHAPE

06-07

LOCATED CLOSE TO
ANOTHER HOUSE DESIGNED
BY THE SAME PRACTICE,
PA1 IS SURROUNDED BY
AN OLD APPLE ORCHARD

08-09

EARLY EXPERIMENTS –
THE ARCHITECTS TRIALLED
THE USE OF POLYURETHANE
FOAM BY COATING LARGE
TUBES FOR THERMAL
INSULATION

Suburban | LENAERTS-THIJS HOUSE
Broekx-Schiepers Architects
Belgium

Hasselt-based architects Jo Broekx and Marcella Schiepers describe the Lenaerts-Thijs house (2006) as one of their favourite projects. The couple were 'personally involved in every part of the design and the construction' of this small house, and the design demonstrates a clear focus on the use of traditional materials, typologies and building techniques.

This single-family house in the village of Meerhout, in Belgium's Antwerp province, uses traditional elements, cleverly adapted to fit the small household's contemporary lifestyle. This conscious decision to avoid 'modern' styles derived as much from the architects' philosophy and site-specific approach, as from the local building regulations, which dictated a classic roof for every residential project in the area.

Broekx and Schiepers used Beerse brick, a type of baked orange-red local clay brick produced in the Antwerp region since 1865. Sustainability and affordability were central in the design's development.

Simplicity was equally important. Having to work with a limited budget, Broekx-Schiepers Architects made the most out of the abstract – almost childlike – conventional shape of a family home. Though small – the entire site area is a mere 230 square metres (2475 square feet), in which the building's footprint corresponds to 80 square metres (860 square feet) for each floor – the house spreads across two levels, taking advantage of a clever and functional interior layout.

From inside, the space feels considerably larger than its actual size. Some of its main spaces, such as the central garden-view room, have double-height ceilings. The house's floor plan is effectively made out of two dislocated square-shaped parts, which form the ground-floor living areas and the first-floor bedrooms, connecting at the garden room's core space. This in-between space, which essentially is the heart of the house's floor plan, spreads vertically across two levels: in this way, the architects succeeded in connecting not only its main parts, but also each level.

The characteristic roof is made of ceramic tiles, and the shape was produced by placing a large conventional roof design on the house, and then cutting out, stretching and folding it to cover all the desired areas, while managing to stay within building regulations. Underneath, the house includes bedrooms, bathrooms, a kitchen featuring a solid beech floor, a living area leading to the garden room and an office space cleverly concealed behind a sliding door. The architects also paid special attention to the interior detailing, creating bespoke handles and banisters, and proving that a small budget does not have to lead to design compromise.

Using local traditional materials such as the rough bricks and the ceramic tiles, and skilfully playing with the volumes and layouts, Broekx-Schiepers maintained a safe distance from current trends and architectural fashions, and designed a functional house based on familiar forms and material honesty.

Suburban | LENAERTS-THIJS HOUSE
Broekx-Schiepers Architects
Belgium

01

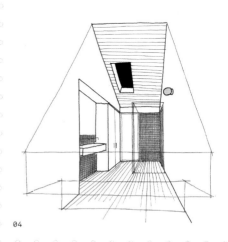

04

02

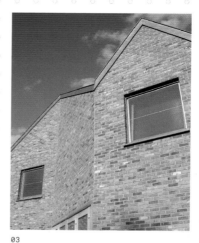

03

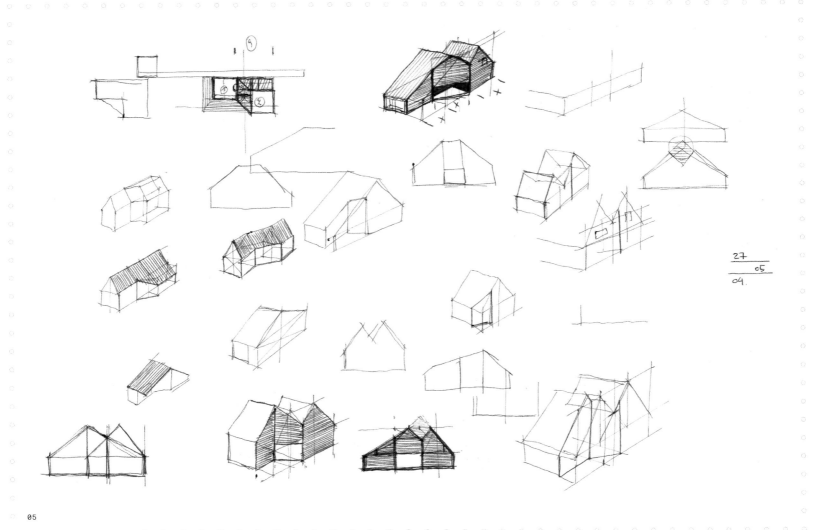

27
05
04.

05

Suburban | LENAERTS-THIJS HOUSE
Broekx-Schiepers Architects
Belgium

06

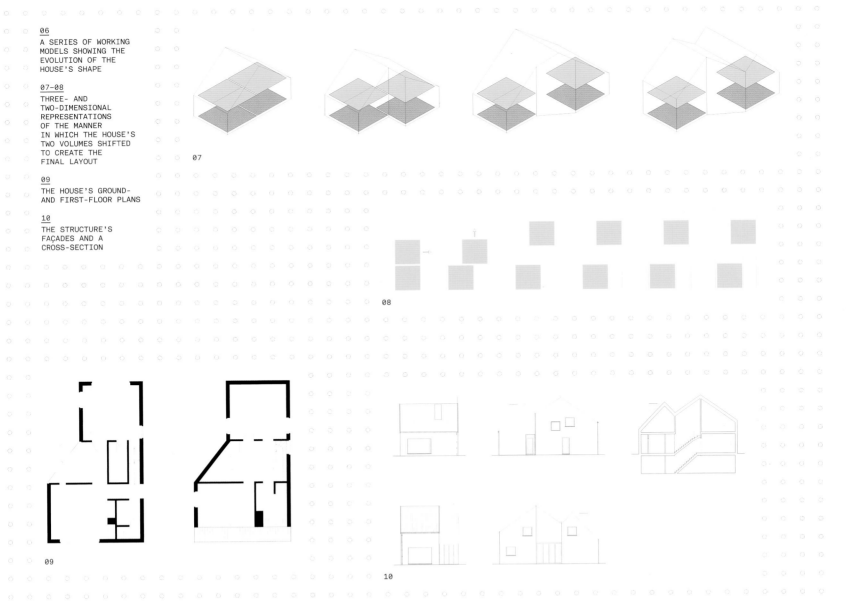

06
A SERIES OF WORKING
MODELS SHOWING THE
EVOLUTION OF THE
HOUSE'S SHAPE

07-08
THREE- AND
TWO-DIMENSIONAL
REPRESENTATIONS
OF THE MANNER
IN WHICH THE HOUSE'S
TWO VOLUMES SHIFTED
TO CREATE THE
FINAL LAYOUT

09
THE HOUSE'S GROUND-
AND FIRST-FLOOR PLANS

10
THE STRUCTURE'S
FAÇADES AND A
CROSS-SECTION

07

08

09

10

Suburban | SINGLE-FAMILY HOUSE
Kamil Mrva Architects
Czech Republic

Sitting next to Dolni Becva city's Beskydy protected area, this single-family vacation house was designed by Czech architect Kamil Mrva for his brother's family in 2006. With the commission coming from a family member, Mrva was lucky enough to have full creative freedom for its design; he describes the project as one of his favourites. Opting for an almost DIY approach in order to accommodate the minute budget and the demands of a small site, the architect was directly involved in all stages of the house's creation, from design to site supervision, and even the actual construction itself.

The project's small physical and economic size was not the only challenge. The proximity of the beautiful old Wallachian town of Roznov pod Radhostem, as well as the surrounding listed buildings, meant the team took about two years to obtain planning permission for a contemporary structure. As a way to demonstrate the new-built house's respect for its protected locale, the architect designed it in a style reminiscent of the wider region's typical historical buildings.

The building is situated in the middle of the plot, its plan running parallel to the site's oblong shape. The house may seem rather small and straightforward in concept and material palette, including entrance hall, living and kitchen area, storage, bathroom and two bedrooms; in fact, the shape is an abstract interpretation of the area's traditional residential architecture.

The main material used is wood, which is this Czech region's favourite construction material. Mrva has a strong background in carpentry, having travelled extensively in Canada to develop his skills, and also has a deep admiration for the simplicity of regional Modernism and its interpretations. Putting his woodworking expertise to use, the architect adopted a hands-on approach in the construction.

Mrva chose natural materials for the exterior skin – larch cladding, combined with modern glazing – with a wooden frame structure, and a simple saddle roof. The relationship of house and site is enhanced by the light wooden terrace on the south side, stretching out straight from the internal living area and visually expanding the space outwards.

Brno-trained Mrva always aims for a site-specific approach, and elements of the local vernacular are often his preferred starting point in a new design. Emphasizing clean shapes and natural materials, and following a 'less is more' mantra, he combines contemporary construction techniques with his love for craft, tradition and woodworking.

LEFT
KAMIL MRVA DESIGNED THIS WOOD-CLAD SINGLE-FAMILY HOUSE FOLLOWING SIMPLE GEOMETRIES AND THE ARCHITECT'S STRONG CARPENTRY EXPERIENCE

ABOVE
THE EXPOSED ROOF BEAMS, EVIDENCE OF THE WOODWORK USED IN THE BUILDING, CONTRAST WITH THE CONTEMPORARY INTERIOR

Suburban | SINGLE-FAMILY HOUSE
Kamil Mrva Architects
Czech Republic

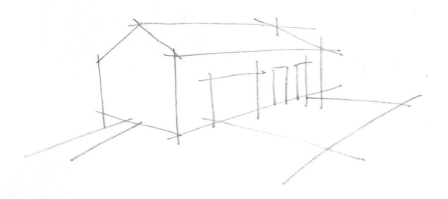

01

01
THE ARCHITECT'S
ULTRA-BASIC CONCEPT
SKETCH FOR THE HOUSE

02
THE HOUSE'S SIMPLE
SHAPES ALLOWED FOR
A STRAIGHTFORWARD AND
QUICK CONSTRUCTION
PROCESS

03
THE HOUSE WAS
CONSTRUCTED USING
A WOODEN FRAME

02

03

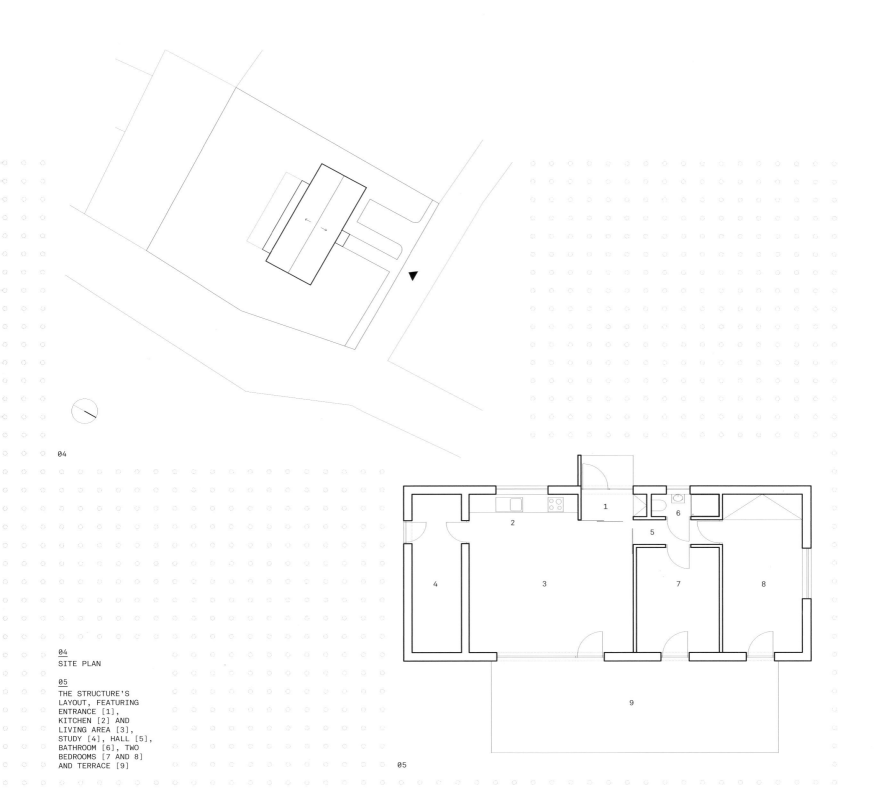

04

05
THE STRUCTURE'S
LAYOUT, FEATURING
ENTRANCE [1],
KITCHEN [2] AND
LIVING AREA [3],
STUDY [4], HALL [5],
BATHROOM [6], TWO
BEDROOMS [7 AND 8]
AND TERRACE [9]

05

Suburban | MIRROR HOUSE
Philippe Gazeau Architecte
France

The Mirror House is a residential project designed by Philippe Gazeau and Michelle Pasquier. The combination of steel and concrete is a deliberate riposte to the 'dullness' of the existing street and the 'ordinary ugliness of the surrounding houses'. The resulting house (2005) is an exercise in translating functional, industrial components and systems into the domestic context.

Faced with a small and relatively unprepossessing site in the western Parisian suburb of Suresnes, the architects treated the street elevation with simplicity, reserving their creativity for the rear of the structure. Describing the form of the house as 'exogenous' – in that it came from outside the system it exists within – Gazeau and Pasquier were chiefly concerned with maintaining a sense of interior space flowing between front and rear façade, even though each elevation has a very different character from the other.

Context therefore defines the public face of the house, with sliding metal screens to protect the client's privacy and an overall sense of shelter against the 'uninteresting neighbourhood'. Content to let the context formulate a tough, almost aggressive building, the architects turned to an almost totally glazed rear façade to create what they describe as a 'strange and ambiguous relationship' between house and garden. The clear glass at ground-floor level gives way to mirrored stainless-steel panels, reflecting and duplicating the surrounding neighbourhood.

The interior planning reflects the garden focus created by the glazed façade, with brightly painted exposed steel elements threaded through the space, denoting the vertical and horizontal cuts through the concrete shell that Gazeau has used to separate the house into different functional zones. Although it is radical in comparison with surrounding houses, the architect is modest about the approach: 'There are no architectural or technical innovations as such, just the fact that each architectural and technical decision has been developed and pushed to its extreme spatial and constructive limits.' Markedly different in scale to PGA's normal output of industrial, education and apartment buildings, the Mirror House combines a high-tech sensibility with complex spatial planning.

THE GARDEN FAÇADE OF THE MIRROR HOUSE, A MIX OF GLAZING AND MIRRORED PANELS, PLAYFULLY REVEALS THE STRUCTURE WHILE ALSO REFLECTING SURROUNDING HOUSES

01

01
A VIEW FROM WITHIN
THE KITCHEN MEZZANINE,
LOOKING OUT OVER THE
LIVING AREA TO THE GARDEN

02
UNDER CONSTRUCTION:
THE CONCRETE CORE OF
THE HOUSE BEFORE GLAZING

03
THE GLAZING ARRANGEMENT
OF THE REAR FAÇADE

02

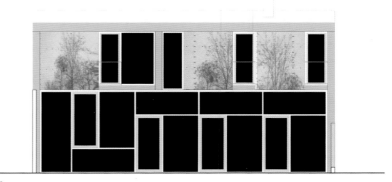

03

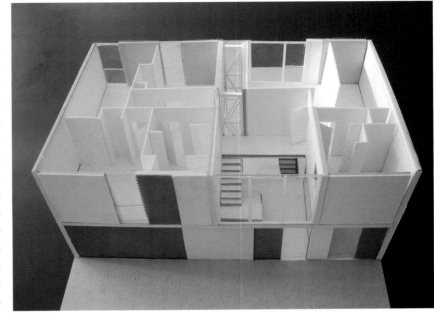

05

04

04
THE MIRROR — THE
CONCEPTUAL HEART
OF THE PROJECT

05
ARCHITECT'S WORKING
MODEL, LOOKING AT THE
FRONT OF THE HOUSE

06
THE LOCATION

06

THIS PAGE
THE BOLD HOUSE CLIENT
ASKED FOR A FUNCTIONAL
DESIGN AND CLEAN
MINIMAL AESTHETICS

OPPOSITE
THE HOUSE OPENS UP TOWARDS
THE LAKE AND MOUNTAIN
VIEWS, WHILE SHUTTING
OFF THE REST OF ITS
SURROUNDINGS BY USING
CONCRETE SIDE FAÇADES

Suburban | BOLD HOUSE
Thomas Bendel
Germany

When a young entrepreneur approached Berlin-based architect Thomas Bendel to design his house in Bodensee, Bendel was intrigued by the challenge. The brief was for a flexible residential space, which would combine work and living spaces as well as functionality and clean aesthetics. The site was situated in a mixed-use zone near Lake Constance, where buildings range from clay-brick residential to commercial, and from small industrial to storage facilities and some offices. The area surrounding the plot is of equally mixed architectural styles, which inspired the architect to go for a slightly different design approach.

Bendel visualized the house as a hollow tube, a strong and simple near-cylindrical surface. Completed in 2005, the two-storey building is divided inside into the ground floor's workspace, including storage and services areas, and the first floor's living spaces, split into two apartments and accompanied by two office spaces. The layout was designed to be as flexible as possible: so, for example, a large sliding door separates or unifies the office space and the living room of the bigger apartment, connecting (or separating) work and leisure. Additionally, should the owner want to use this apartment for commercial purposes, the spaces can be adjusted, and the foyer enlarged, by simply removing a light separating wall.

The building's outside space is also carefully planned, subdivided into clearly defined areas of tar, grit or lawn. Black aluminium roller shutters help to control the relationship of inside and outside, while the terrace, created by removing an orthogonal block from the building's upper level, acts as an open patio in the centre of the apartment.

The structure's main materials are as simple and clear as its concept; reinforced concrete for the overall envelope, glass and black anodized aluminium for the sides, which 'seal' the tube's two ends. 'The bright open area requires archaic forms and basic material; they affiliate with the landscape,' the architect writes.

The tube form was a very conscious choice. By opening up two sides of the volume, and closing carefully the other two, Bendel has oriented the house to look towards the stunning natural landscape views – the lake and the Bavarian mountains – and turn its back to the surrounding uninspired architectural mix. That shape and orientation also serve to protect the house from the strong winds created in the open, un-built plain between the structure and the lake.

Both the materials and the shapes used to realize his concept reflect Bendel's main philosophy and design aspirations, concentrating as he does on the bare essentials. Combining these values with a site-specific approach, and of course the available budget's flexibility, the architect designed a house and workspace that has simplicity as its basis, but a simplicity supplemented where needed with elaborate details and calculated planning.

01

02

01
THE HOUSE'S SHAPE IS ESSENTIALLY PART OF A TUBE, WITH TWO OPEN SIDES AND TWO BLIND ONES

02
THE UPPER-FLOOR INTERIOR IS SIMPLE AND CAN BE USED AS OFFICE OR LIVING SPACE

03
THE HOUSE'S SECTION SHOWS HOW THE TWO LEVELS AND THE DIFFERENT USES CONNECT SPATIALLY

04–05
THE ARCHITECT'S PRELIMINARY SKETCHES GIVE AN INSIGHT TO THE HOUSE'S TUBE-LIKE FINAL SHAPE AND EXPLAIN THE BIRTH OF THE UPPER-FLOOR ATRIUM

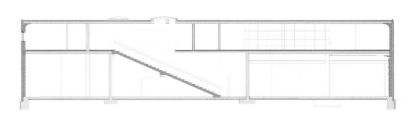

03

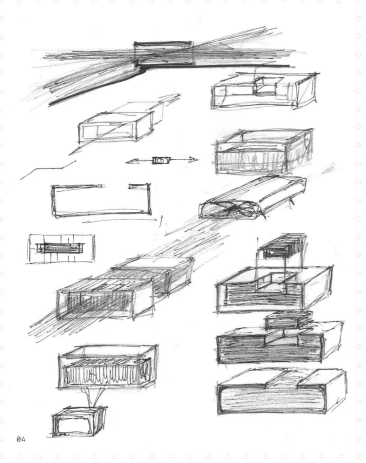

04

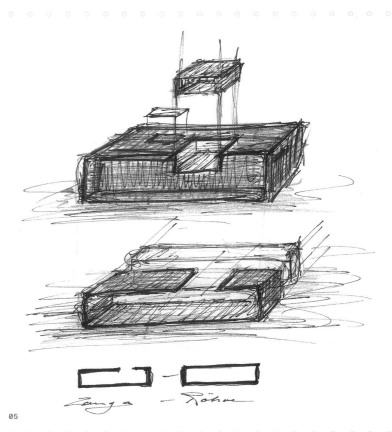

05

Suburban | 9X9 HOUSE
Titus Bernhard Architekten
Germany

9x9 House is located in the small suburban community of Titus Bernhard's hometown of Augsburg, in south-west Bavaria. The pitched-roof silhouette may be familiar, but this two-storey residence (2003) became the cause of considerable controversy after the architect applied for planning permission at the local municipal building authorities and endured a lengthy battle with local bureaucracy.

Bernhard used the commission for a couple's family home to make a statement about this traditionally minded area's resistance to innovative architecture. Conceiving the whole building as an inhabitable sculpture, Bernhard responded to the existing built environment by challenging the local inhabitants' idea of a 'conventional' single-family house.

The site measures 9 x 9 metres (30 x 30 feet), providing the architect with a clean square shape for the house, which he topped with an asymmetrical pyramidal roof. The building's most unconventional feature is undoubtedly its rough exterior shell, which is made of thousands of stones in wire baskets, known as gabions, a technique more usually found in retaining walls. 9x9 House is the first residential building designed in this way; the gabion façade is suspended from the insulated, sealed shell as a non-load-bearing structure, while the house's main framework is concrete.

Not only do the design's aesthetic claims come second to the house's functional needs and overall status as a statement, but it also follows an ecological approach. The house's entire shell is contained within the cages, which act as a second skin and wrap around the walls and roof. This layer of stone functions as a hydrophilic structure, meaning that the building absorbs water without allowing internal leakage, and thereby does not need rainwater pipes or drainage systems. The cages were filled by hand with about 40,000 stones, creating a total 28-tonne mass around the house. Throughout the year, this volume regulates thermal transfer, which stabilizes the interior temperatures to comfortable living levels, keeping extra heating requirements to a minimum.

The house's basic geometric shape hosts an open-plan interior, including living, dining and kitchen areas, bedrooms, bathrooms, wardrobe space, and a reading and a work gallery, over two floors and an attic. Contrasting the house's tough exterior, the pale plastered interior's design produces an airy, comfortable feel in the rooms, also securing plenty of natural light.

In introducing this innovative, ecological and cost-effective building and insulating technique, the architect enjoyed the continuous support of the owners, and produced a visually striking, inexpensive and energy-sustainable result. The bold, succinct design encouraged the participating materials suppliers to contribute up to 70 per cent of the façade's costs.

Suburban | 9X9 HOUSE
Titus Bernhard Architekten
Germany

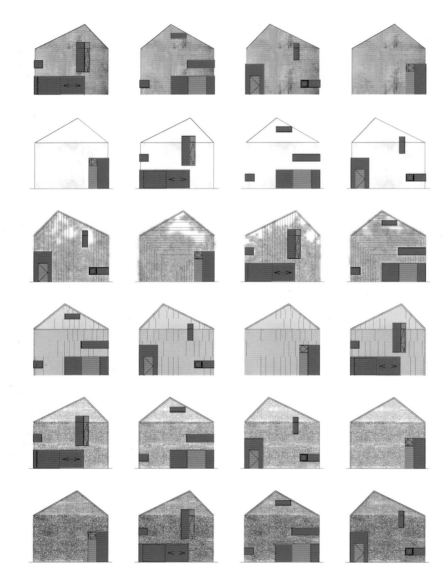

01

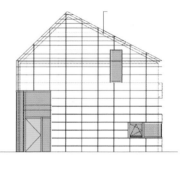

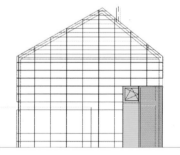

02

01
STUDIES OF SEVERAL
DIFFERENT MATERIALS
LED TO THE EVENTUAL
STONE-WALL SOLUTION

02
THE HOUSE'S NORTH
(TOP) AND EAST
(BOTTOM) FAÇADES

03
STAGES IN THE
CONSTRUCTION
OF 9X9 HOUSE

03

Suburban | SILENT HOUSE
Takao Shiotsuka Atelier
Japan

LEFT
THE MODESTLY MINIMAL
SILENT HOUSE IS SET
AMID KYUSHU'S RICH
NATURAL LANDSCAPE

RIGHT
THE HOUSE'S INTERIOR
IS AS SIMPLE AND MONASTIC
AS ITS EXTERIOR

Located on the north-eastern side of Kyushu Island, in Japan's Oita prefecture, Saiki City is a fast-growing town, the second largest on the island. The hectic urban location was one of the key reasons – although certainly not the only one – why local architect Takao Shiotsuka approached a new residential commission just outside the city limits with the concept of silence foremost in his mind.

The site, destined to house the city-dwelling client's much-needed holiday retreat, overlooks the mountains and the area's rich vegetation. The client's grandfather used to live in a small wooden house on the same spot and the family grave is also located next to the plot. The new structure would serve both as a holiday home and as a place used by all the relatives during religious events in honour of their ancestors' souls.

Shiotsuka conceived the house as a 'cottage in the silent village between mountains', a place that would induce peace of mind in its inhabitants. Appropriately 'quiet' and modest in design, as well as small in size, the cottage took only about a year to finish from the first design stages to the final construction details.

The house's orthogonal volume came out of a series of tests and studies of smaller spaces within spaces. The living areas are spread across three smaller interior units, placed within a single larger orthogonal envelope, both inner and outer constructions made of concrete blocks. This way, the architect was able to create a semi-open corridor circulating the house, adding an extra layer, which also shields the inhabitants from the outside world. The height differences in the roof reflect the internal layout, corresponding to each of the house's rooms. The cottage covers basic residential functions, featuring bedroom, bathroom, and a unified living and kitchen area on the ground level, as well as a small loft.

The one-level cottage, completed in 2008, extends to just over 80 square metres (860 square feet) of total floor space. The rough concrete blocks were chosen as the structure's main building material simply because they instinctively felt like a discreet and 'silent' material. Stacking them carefully to create walls, Shiotsuka has left generous openings to frame the beautiful views and to enhance the natural lighting. The external skin's doors and windows are frameless and entirely open, with the intention of making the house appear as minimal and unobtrusive in the landscape as possible. Using concrete-finished ceilings, and either cedar strip or Japanese tatami-style flooring, the materials inside the house are equally basic, and include wood from the nearby forest.

Seeking to express silence through reductivist design, Shiotsuka responded to the beauty of the cottage's surroundings, a humble and peaceful village in the green Japanese countryside, while meeting the client's requirements for a serene and private retreat. The cottage's almost primitive structure shies away from material luxuries, expressing humility, peace and tranquillity through its combination of functional materials and minimal detailing, connecting to both context and family history.

Suburban | SILENT HOUSE
Takao Shiotsuka Atelier
Japan

01

03

02

04

01
THE FINAL MODEL
OF SILENT HOUSE

02
THE AREA'S TRADITIONAL
STONE RETAINING WALLS
SURROUND THE SITE

03
BASIC CONCRETE BLOCKS
WERE THE HOUSE'S MAIN
STRUCTURAL COMPONENTS

04
THE SILENT HOUSE'S
FLAT PLOT, NEXT
TO A ZELKOVA TREE,
MADE MARKING THE
FOUNDATION LINES AND
PREPARING THE GROUND
FOR THE CONSTRUCTION
WORKS EASIER

SHIOTSUKA EXPERIMENTED
WITH SEVERAL DIFFERENT
SHAPES BEFORE CHOOSING
THE HOUSE'S FINAL
RECTANGULAR FORM

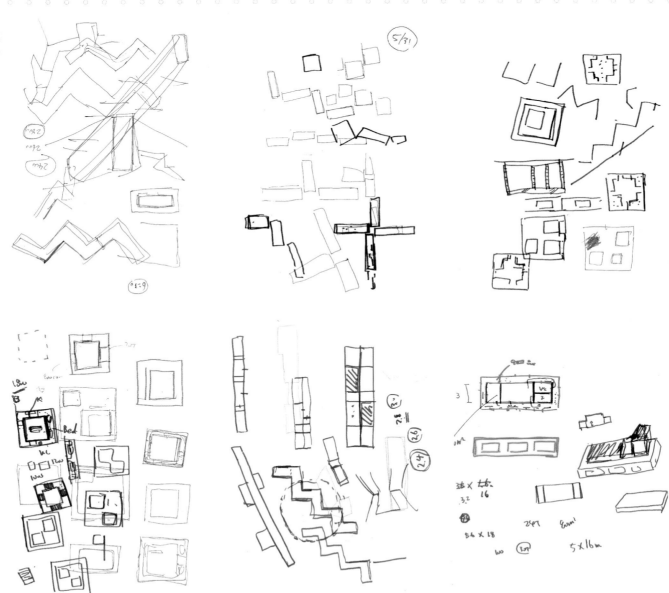

05

Suburban PRIVATE HOUSE
ARHIS
Latvia

ARHIS's house in the Melluzi area of Jurmala, designed by Andris Kronbergs, Ansis Zitars and Barbara Abele, is the extensive reconstruction of a 1950s building. While markedly different from the local vernacular (characterized by ornamented gables, turrets and traditional carpentry), the Jurmala house retains essential original details – such as the central staircase ('a testimony of the mastery of a previous generation of Jurmala carpenters') and fireplace, the latter shifted from being a fundamental part of the house's function to a focal point for family gathering.

The external 'skin' of grey boarding serves to unify the massing of the house, giving a modern look to what is in effect a very conventional form. The use of the same material on both walls and roof, together with a walkway that runs right around the house, helps to draw attention to the deep-set windows, the depth of the reveal demonstrating how flimsy and frail the original, uninsulated structure was. At the rear, a glazed conservatory cube opens up the living space to the garden. The reconstruction also allowed for the creation of a new studio space in the attic, an open-plan space at odds with the traditionally small rooms of the old house.

The grey skin was chosen for the way it evokes the tarred and weathered hulls of the traditional fishermen's boats, once arranged en masse on the shores of the Gulf of Riga along which the resort of Jurmala spreads out. Like Simon Conder's rubber-clad house in Dungeness, England, the house in Jurmala is a modern interpretation of an abandoned aesthetic, battered by natural forces and economic shifts. The architects write that 'the house's identity and its specific qualities distinguish it from most of the other Jurmala development and make it more similar to a fisherman's farmstead from the last century'. The house was completed in 2007.

LOCATED IN A WOODED SITE IN JURMALA, THIS RECONSTRUCTION OF A TYPICAL 1950S HOUSE OVERCLADS AND EXTENDS THE ORIGINAL PROPERTY TO DRAMATIC EFFECT

Suburban | PRIVATE HOUSE
ARHIS
Latvia

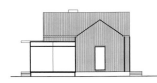

01

02

03

01

ELEVATIONS, SHOWING
HOW THE ORIGINAL
STORY STRUCTURE HAS
BEEN 'WRAPPED' BY
THE EXTENSIONS

02

TWO VIEWS OF THE
ORIGINAL HOUSE

03

THE ADDITIONS ADD
SPACE AND TRANSFORM
THE AESTHETIC OF
THE HOUSE, WITH
LARGE EXPANSES OF
GLAZING AND DARK,
SOMBRE CLADDING

04

DESIGN SKETCHES:
THE GUTTERING AND ROOF
PITCH DETAILS HELP
TO CREATE THE HOUSE'S
SEAMLESS APPEARANCE

05

DESIGN SKETCHES
EXPLORING THE
RELATIONSHIP BETWEEN
OLD AND NEW VOLUMES

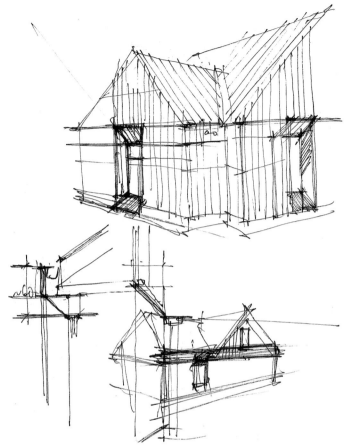

04

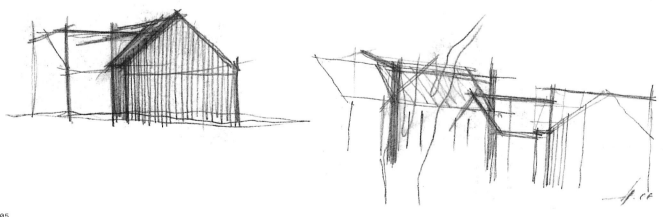

05

THIS PAGE
WOLZAK HOUSE INCLUDES
AN IRREGULARLY SHAPED
EXTENSION TO THE EXISTING
FARMHOUSE BUILDINGS

OPPOSITE
SKETCH SHOWING THE
NEW WING SITTING NEXT
TO THE OLDER BUILDINGS

Suburban | WOLZAK HOUSE
SeARCH
The Netherlands

The Dutch architects SeARCH have been specializing in architectural conversion and creative reuse for most of their career, often working on several such residential projects at one time. They are familiar with the appeals and challenges of transforming an old abandoned farmyard into a family's dream home, and their 2004–2005 Wolzak House project defines their approach to this category.

The house project, commissioned by a young local family, involved an old T-shaped farm building in Zutphen, in the east of the country. The architects wanted to avoid treating the old and the new wing in different ways by designing the family house and the shed as two separate spaces. Instead, they redesigned certain parts and expanded the complex, aiming to create a structure with a strong single identity. In order to achieve this, they began by replacing the old farm's livestock barn with a new wing for the house, aiming to treat it as an integral part of the home.

Principal Bjarne Mastenbroek and his team chose to retain the refurbished older building's thatched roof – above the main living spaces of the complex – in order to keep the complex's historical continuity. The main farm building was perfectly restored and fitted with all the necessary equipment for a modern family house. However, the new volume was not as conventional, having a tilted shape that was the result of a drag-and-

pull perspective distortion. Nonetheless, visually and in plan, it still served as one part of the traditional T-shape of the historic complex.

The new building is constructed using prefabricated wood plates: contained beneath its steep roof are a large open-plan kitchen space and the house's main entrance, as well as a workroom, guest room and storage area. A large conservatory on the garden side also includes the main entrance and separates visually the kitchen and dining areas from the rest of the house. By using timber in various forms throughout the complex, and especially in the redesigned part, the architects created a sense of unity. While the roof and elevations are all clad in horizontal timber laths, wood is also used in the interior, the detailing and finishes.

Nearby is a detached barn, which was originally planned to house the guest rooms. The final plan incorporated these into the main complex, so the barn is now designated for a future indoor swimming pool.

The house combines old and new, and open and closed spaces, and offers a pleasantly distorted version of a farmhouse complex, retaining a sense of history and, most importantly, creating a single dynamic structure under a consistent architectural approach.

01

02

03

<u>01</u>
SIDE VIEW OF
THE NEW WING

<u>02-03</u>
TWO STUDY MODELS
PRESENTING THE
ARCHITECTS'
EXPERIMENTATION WITH
SHAPES AND MATERIALS

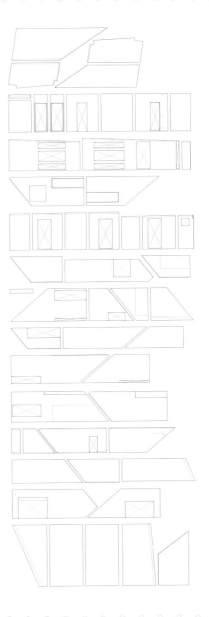

04

04
HAND-DRAWN SIDE
FAÇADE OF THE EXISTING
BARN STRUCTURE AND THE
NEW WING

05
AERIAL VIEW OF
THE COMPLEX

06
THE HOUSE'S KIT OF
PREFABRICATED ELEMENTS

05

06

Suburban | TRIANGLE HOUSE
JVA
Norway

For architects it is standard practice to take into account a site's surroundings in the design procedure, together with any local rules or guidelines regarding the height, length and width of a building. In the case of the Triangle House (2006), Norwegian architects JVA (Jarmund/Vigsnæs AS Arkitekter) were prepared to set their own additional limits. The plot is located in Nesodden, less than an hour from Oslo, on the top of a hill overlooking the sea through a dense pine forest. The house's particular shape was largely dictated by the surrounding trees' branches, which entered the site from all sides, defining the building lines and consequently the house's triangular shape.

Echoing traditional Norwegian building styles, the house was simply and modestly clad in wood inside and out. The exterior is clad with wood panels, the interior with OSB (oriented strand board), while floors are made from cast concrete and the bathrooms feature brushed aluminium panes and mirrors.

While the house seems severe and angular from the outside, the interior layout is anything but. Free-flowing open plans were used throughout, bringing bright light into the whole of the interior, with spaces that communicate both horizontally and vertically. Meanwhile, the views towards the forest and through to the sea are beautifully framed by the carefully located window openings.

The interior is further transformed by the owners' sizeable library, which has been housed on floor-to-ceiling shelves in the main living spaces, also helping to soften the acoustics. 'The owners say that they sleep very well in this house,' the architects claim – in a space at one with its site and with the local environment.

LEFT
THE LIGHT-FILLED LIVING AREA INCLUDES EXTENSIVE BUILT-IN SHELVING

OPPOSITE
WITH LARGE, STRATEGICALLY PLACED SLICED-OPEN WINDOWS ALLOWING VIEWS TOWARDS THE SEA THROUGH THE PINE FOREST, THE BULK OF THE TRIANGLE HOUSE'S EXTERIOR IS CLAD IN WOOD PANELS

Suburban | TRIANGLE HOUSE
JVA
Norway

01
SITE PLAN SHOWING
THE HOUSE'S LOCATION
WITHIN THE PLOT

02–03
TWO OF THE TRIANGLE
HOUSE'S FINAL MODELS

04
THE HOUSE'S SOUTH
ELEVATION

05
THE STRUCTURE'S
GROUND-FLOOR PLAN

06
THE HOUSE'S EAST
FAÇADE FEATURES AN
UPPER-FLOOR TERRACE,
WHICH WAS CREATED
BY CARVING OFF A
TRIANGULAR SHARD FROM
THE TOP OF THE VOLUME'S
EAST CORNER

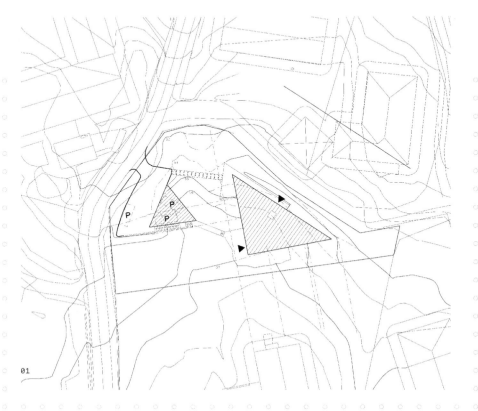

01

02

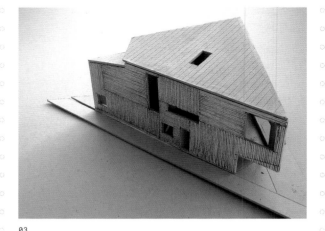

03

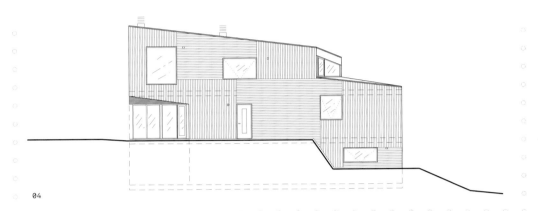

04

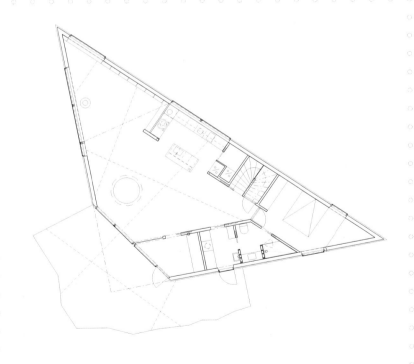

05

06

Suburban | STUDIOHOUSE IN BÜSSERACH
Degelo Architekten
Switzerland

THE NORTH FAÇADE
REVEALS THE MOST
STRIKING FEATURE OF
DEGELO ARCHITEKTEN'S
COMPREHENSIVE
CONVERSION: A PICTURE
WINDOW THAT OPENS
UP VIEWS FROM THE
UPPER FLOOR. THE
PITCHED ROOF IS CLAD
IN UNTREATED STEEL

A conversion of an existing storage shed and workshop, Degelo Architekten's Studiohouse (2007) remakes the original prosaic structure into a live/work space, a major intervention undertaken with a minimalist's touch. The addition of a new roof structure enabled the pitch to be enhanced with an additional dormer section to create a full-height third storey of accommodation. In direct reference to local agricultural buildings, the roof is clad in untreated steel plates, which are being allowed to slowly acquire a patina of rust.

The ground floor is of concrete construction; like the rest of the building, the surfaces and finishes are left raw and exposed wherever possible. On the first floor, large openings have been made for the insertion of frameless floor-to-ceiling windows, which provide panoramic views of the surrounding landscape. The timber-clad exterior is echoed inside by fir boards cladding the walls and ceiling, while the downstairs studio space has waxed cement walls and a cast plaster floor. The new attic space – also a studio – has a vast picture window facing north.

Finished without skirtings, cornices or rails, the interior is austere, with doors and openings pushed to the edge of the floor plan to maximize the interplay between the different planes – floors, wall and ceiling. A red-painted stair between the first and second floors stands as a sculptural object in the high-ceilinged space.

The Studiohouse is a lesson in patination, a process seemingly at odds with the crisp newness that once defined modern architecture. The sense that materials and objects have innate qualities that change and improve with age and use is not usually addressed in contemporary architecture, where the lasting impression of a building is invariably an image that is taken almost immediately after completion; the Modern building remains fixed and immutable, eternally new and unoccupied.

By bringing together a combination of the existing structure and new materials chosen for their ageing qualities, the Studiohouse, like many other projects featured here, acknowledges the transitory nature of newness right from the outset.

161

Felix Jerusalem's Compressed Straw House is an experimental structure designed to demonstrate the performance of new forms of building material. Completed in 2005, the single-storey family house in Eschenz utilizes prefabricated solid panels, filled with highly compressed straw as insulation. Jerusalem is an educator as well as an architect, and has taught at the Eidgenössische Technische Hochschule in Zürich. Clarity of vision is central to his personal architectural work, as well as ongoing discussions between students, faculty and visiting architects.

The 'Strohhaus' is unashamedly Modernist in form in the contemporary Swiss tradition, partly raised up on concrete pillars to protect the archaeologically rich fabric of the surrounding site. A concrete structure was infilled with the specially developed panels to form the external walls and internal partitions. A poured slab floor contains the underfloor heating elements. The prefabricated panels are clad in a translucent weather shield, a skin of corrugated panels made from fibreglass-reinforced polyester resins and manufactured by the Swiss company Scobalit. This reflects the external light and animates the façade depending on the time of day.

The entire accommodation is arranged on a single storey beneath the mono-pitched roof, which rises sufficiently to create a galleried area at one end. Services are contained with the central concrete core and include a bathroom and heating controls. A galley kitchen is 'docked' to this service core, and it also burrows into the ground beneath the house so as to create a small wine-cellar. Two children's bedrooms are located at the thin end of the wedge shape, while the parents' room is set at the other end. Everything else is open-plan, with a suspended black fireplace pod in the double-height living space marking a stark contrast with the white and yellow colour scheme of the interior.

The environmental benefits of deriving building materials from a common crop are obvious, and the panels use plant fibres as the basis of both structure and insulation. The panels were manufactured in Germany and are modular in construction and variable in density, depending on how much the straw is compressed; single boards of up to 6 x 2.5 metres (20 x 8 feet) can be produced. The panels are free of formaldehyde and the production process is low in emissions. The crops best suited to producing the straw are rice and bamboo; straw is a waste product in rice production. The combination of weather shield and straw panel makes for a very thermally efficient structure.

Design and theoretical inspiration included Marcel Breuer's houses in New England, the work of Basel architect Paul Artaria, and the Farnsworth House by Mies van der Rohe, particularly in the spatial planning of the service core and kitchen. Although developed as a practical exercise to experiment with a new material, the House in Eschenz transcends its experimental origins to form an innovative family dwelling with a minimal plan.

FELIX JERUSALEM'S EXPERIMENTAL FAMILY HOUSE USES COMPRESSED STRAW PANELS, OVERCLAD WITH TRANSLUCENT POLYCARBONATE, FOR THE EXTERNAL FAÇADE. RAISED ABOVE ITS SUBURBAN SITE, THE SINGLE-STOREY HOUSE HAS A CONCRETE CORE

Suburban | COMPRESSED STRAW HOUSE
Felix Jerusalem
Switzerland

THIS PAGE
THE WINDOW REVEALS
ILLUSTRATE THE DEPTH OF
THE WALLS; THE HOUSE IS
HEAVILY INSULATED USING A
LOW-COST, ENVIRONMENTALLY
FRIENDLY STRAW-PANEL
CONSTRUCTION

OPPOSITE
THE CONCRETE SLAB AND
CORE ARE CONTRASTED WITH
YELLOW WALLS AND SIMPLE
DETAILS, SUCH AS THIS
SUSPENDED STOVE. A STAIR
AT THE LEFT LEADS UP TO
THE MEZZANINE

Suburban | COMPRESSED STRAW HOUSE
Felix Jerusalem
Switzerland

01

02

04

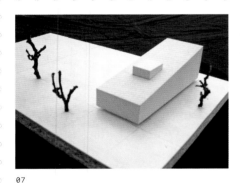

05

03

06

07

08

01-03
STRAW BALE
CONSTRUCTION IS
FAR FROM BEING A
NEW CONCEPT

04-06
THE HIGHLY COMPRESSED
STRAW PANELS CAN BE
MANUFACTURED IN A
VARIETY OF SIZES

07-08
EARLY MASSING STUDIES
INDICATE THE EVENTUAL
WEDGE-SHAPED FORM OF
THE HOUSE

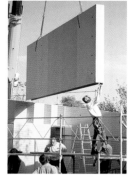

09

10

11

09–11
STRAW PANELS ARE
RAISED INTO PLACE,
WITH THE CENTRAL
CONCRETE CORE
PROVIDING THE GUIDE

12–14
THE TRANSLUCENT
FAÇADE WAS INSPIRED
BY SUNLIGHT ON WATER.
IT CREATES A
CONSTANTLY SHIFTING
PATTERN OF LIGHT

15
ELEVATIONS. THE
HOUSE WAS INSPIRED
BY THE CLASSIC
MODERNIST PAVILION

12

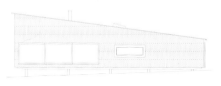

13

14

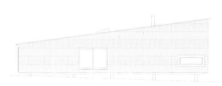

15

167

Suburban | FARADAY HOUSE
Jomini Zimmermann Architects and Thomas Jomini Architecture Workshop
Switzerland

Designed by Swiss architects Thomas Jomini and Jomini Zimmermann Architects (Valérie Jomini and Stanislas Zimmermann), the Faraday House (2004) is located in a suburb of Berne and exemplifies the area's ongoing architectural changes. The district of Lorraine is an area of old workers' houses – a mix of clapboard houses, post-war buildings and a few renovations – which is now swiftly evolving into an 'alternative' urban village of various architectural styles. The architects understood that this would be fertile ground for architectural experimentation.

A house that will shelter its inhabitants not only from the weather but also from electromagnetic fields is aptly named Faraday House, after the 19th-century pioneering researcher into magnetic fields, Michael Faraday. The team rigorously researched the structure's engineering and technologies and provided it with excellent insulation, as well as with a distinctive, electromagnetism-shielding outer layer of copper, intended to protect the inhabitants from the electromagnetic fields coming from the electricity-producing energy park across the neighbouring river. They also designed it with a controlled ventilation system, meeting the Swiss Minergie Standards for low-energy-consumption building. Extra ecological features include a ground-source heat pump, connected to a 180 metre (590 foot) drilling in the ground, used for the house's heating and cooling.

Apart from its technological advantages, the exterior skin also plays a significant role in the structure's appearance. The same material is wrapped all around the house, equally covering the walls as well as the roof. 'We wanted to show the roof as one more façade. That is why we used one material to cover all sides of the house,' says Valérie Jomini. Owing to the way the copper will age, the house's exterior will gradually change from dark brown to light green over a period of two to three decades. The architects treated the façades as ever-changing sensitive interfaces, where time and the elements can all imprint their passing. As time goes by, the house will slowly transform.

The building's playful shape is based partly on a conventional house outline, with the dynamic additions of three smaller volumes protruding from the archetypal form: the staircase, a light shaft at the top and a balcony on the first floor. The Faraday House's interior spaces are fluid and open, and comprise two apartments each spread across two floors. Each apartment is designed to allow for openings on every level towards the best orientation possible. In contrast with the exterior's striking, colourful, curvy character, the interior is much more calm and neutral, full of white clean walls, glass and smooth naked concrete; all materials are used in their true nature, left untreated as much as possible.

The house was completed in 2004. Employing ecological methods, combined with an inventive as well as pragmatic approach to the idea of the house as a shield or a shelter, the architects have designed a quietly innovative house. A sensual and at the same time practical exterior works successfully as a whole with the comfortable residential interior it encloses and protects.

Suburban | FARADAY HOUSE
Jomini Zimmermann Architects and
Thomas Jomini Architecture Workshop
Switzerland

02

01

03

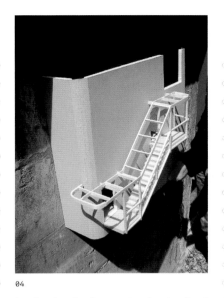

04

05

06

07

THE STREET FAÇADE OF
BBM'S SPARROW HOUSE
ILLUSTRATES THE LONG
PLAN, SET BACK BEHIND
A FRONT GARDEN, WITH
A CENTRALLY PLACED
COURTYARD. THE MONO-PITCH
ROOF IS AT ODDS WITH
NEIGHBOURING HOUSES
BUT NOT DELIBERATELY
ANTAGONISTIC

Suburban | SPARROW HOUSE
BBM Sustainable Design
UK

The aesthetics of low-energy building are generally considered to be a distraction from the real purpose of sustainability, effectively marginalizing the development of sustainable architecture. Rather than entering the mainstream, eco design has been labelled a fringe activity with values and processes that run contrary both to the 'progressive' role of avant-garde architecture and to contextual harmony. BBM Sustainable Design, a small Sussex-based studio, has dedicated itself to dispelling this notion, establishing a series of ground rules for energy-efficient building, from studying usage patterns through to optimizing form and materials.

The Sparrow House in Lewes (2005) was designed by Duncan Baker-Brown for his own family. The long, narrow plot had a history of failed planning applications, as proposals threatened to overdevelop the site or dominate the neighbouring bungalows. By proposing a slender house that used the depth of the site, 6 metres (20 feet) wide and 17 metres (56 feet) long, BBM Sustainable Design finally gained approval from the local authority, although the two-storey façade that faces the road was allowed only after the architects dug down into the site to lower the height of the roof ridge.

Sparrow House is arranged around a central courtyard, surrounded on three sides by glazed folding doors. From the entrance hall, one enters a kitchen/ dining area, with a mezzanine level above providing a sleeping platform and bathroom. Progressing through the living space, one can either walk through the galley kitchen that forms the house's spine and leads to two bedrooms and a bathroom at the rear, or access the garden via the courtyard through large glazed doors.

Orientation determined the plan – the courtyard faces south so solar gain could be maximized – and every detail was developed to minimize material use and the need for excessive mechanical systems. Roof-mounted thermal solar panels provide hot water to the underfloor heating, while lambswool insulation gives the house a high thermal rating. Materials are recyclable or locally sourced wherever possible. Locally grown sweet chestnut wood has been extensively used for the internal joinery, structural frames and external cladding, while recycled scaffolding boards are reused as kitchen worktops.

Through careful planning, BBM has made the most of what it describes as an 'unwanted plot' – land that was not suited to conventional building forms. The combination of white render and wooden cladding gives the house a modest, unassuming appearance, although the concealed pitch of the roof and metal-framed windows imply a modern sensibility, a new visual agenda that hints at its sustainable qualifications.

Suburban | SPARROW HOUSE
BBM Sustainable Design
UK

01
SITE SECTION: THE HOUSE
STEPS DOWN FROM THE STREET,
WITH A MEZZANINE LEVEL AT
THE FRONT, AND THE KITCHEN
AND LIVING AREA ENCIRCLING
THE CENTRAL COURTYARD

02-04
THE HOUSE USES LOCAL
MATERIALS WHEREVER
POSSIBLE, INCLUDING SWEET
CHESTNUT WOOD, LAMBSWOOL
INSULATION AND RECYCLED
SCAFFOLDING BOARDS

05
ROOF-MOUNTED SOLAR PANELS
SUPPLY HOT WATER FOR THE
UNDERFLOOR HEATING

06-10
CONSTRUCTION: THE HOUSE IS
CONVENTIONALLY BUILT USING
A COMBINATION OF STRUCTURAL
STEEL AND WOODEN FRAMING

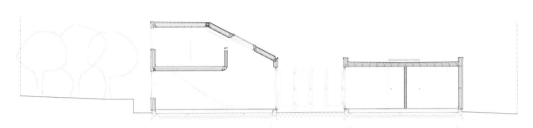

01

03

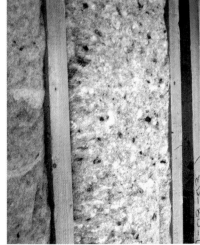

02

04

05

06

07

09

10

08

175

Suburban | XS, S, M, L HOUSES
UNI Architects
USA

For architects Chaewon Kim and her husband Beat Schenk, the design and construction of their house in Massachusetts became an urgent goal after Kim was diagnosed with cancer in 2002, at only 26 years of age. Their budget allowed them to buy a small house in Cambridge, Massachusetts, built in 1894 and measuring just 66 square metres (712 square feet); crucially, though, it was blessed with a large plot, with enough space for an extension and landscaping.

The existing house was a typical vernacular family house, an orthogonal structure with a roof. The couple chose to keep the original form, which they gutted – hauling away almost 10 tonnes of debris – in order to transform the old structure into a functional and cosy contemporary home.

Keen followers of ecology and sustainable systems, the architects decided to work in as environmentally conscious a way as possible. They removed all the old asbestos shingles, insulated the building properly and created large openings and an open-plan layout in order to help the air circulate easier and to bring in as much light as possible. The floor was covered with soft yet durable natural cork tiles, a particularly environmentally friendly material that also has good insulation qualities. All other materials and finishings were kept to a bare minimum – not even mouldings or trims were used. The roof and most of the exterior walls were clad in Corten steel, left unpainted, while the east façade was all glass, to enhance daylight in the house and to open up the views towards the garden.

The structure – named S (for Small) House and now used as the couple's office – was so successful that an extension to the complex – the black box dubbed M – was soon started. After selling M, another two buildings followed on the tight site, both constructed in 2006: the cedar-shingle-covered L, into which the couple moved, and finally, XS. Kim overcame her cancer, with this building project becoming a central focus of her long recovery.

The striking form of the XS addition was created by rotating three stacked boxes on a vertical axis, creating a tower with four corner skylights on each floor. The building is otherwise intriguingly almost windowless, lit via the skylights and a small number of thin slots slashed into the 4.8 x 6.7 metre (16 x 22 foot) volumes, finished in nautical-grade plywood. A large wooden staircase unites all the levels and is placed in the middle of the plan, almost as a sculptural centrepiece. Each floor has its own material identity, featuring sleek marble on the ground level and warm oak plywood on the first and second floors.

The four-volume compound finally reached completion in the early autumn of 2006; the house-turned-office's final cost was about 50 per cent less than the average renovation works in the area. Placed together, S, M, L and finally the iconic XS House, provide an ecologically sustainable constellation of highly affordable residential and commercial space.

Suburban | XS, S, M, L HOUSES
UNI Architects
USA

01

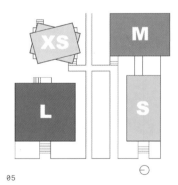

02

03

MODULE

The module/block is the basic constructive element of the modern home with a panelized building system. It can be easily handled, transported and stored as either fully-fitted modules or flat-packed panels.

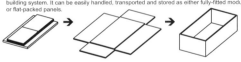

MODULAR CONSTRUCTION

Individual modules are stacked on top of each other. By rotating and shifting modules, multiful skylight can be created to gain more natural light and privacy at narrow lots where homes are located side-by-side closely.

Jenga

Lego

skylight

skylight

skylight

Stack them the way you want to create skylights!

VARIATIONS

by configuration

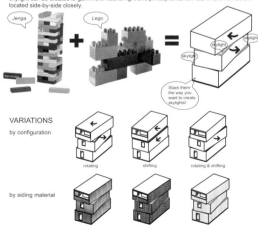

rotating

shifting

rotating & shifting

by siding material

exterior plywood (Prodema)

self-rusting metal (Corten)

translucent polycarbonate (Polygal)

04

XS

M

L

S

05

01-03
A STACK OF JAPANESE
BENTO BOXES INSPIRED
THE UNUSUAL SHAPE OF
THE XS HOUSE

04
SKETCH BY THE
ARCHITECTS PRESENTING
THE MODULE, WHICH
WAS STACKED AND
TWISTED IN ORDER TO
RESULT IN THE XS
HOUSE'S FINAL VOLUME

05
SITE VIEW OF THE
WHOLE PLOT, FEATURING
ALL FOUR STRUCTURES

06
M HOUSE'S WOOD-CLAD
VOLUME SITS RIGHT
BEHIND S HOUSE

07
M HOUSE, LOCATED
AT THE REAR OF THE
SITE, WAS SOLD BY
THE ARCHITECTS
AFTER COMPLETION

06

07

08

09

10

<u>08,10</u>
WOOD FEATURES IN
SEVERAL XS HOUSE
ELEMENTS, FROM THE
CENTRAL STAIRCASE
TO ITS UPPER-FLOOR
INTERIOR SKIN

<u>09</u>
EACH HOUSE IN THE
COMPLEX IS CLAD IN A
DIFFERENT MATERIAL
— DISTINCT WOOD TYPES
FOR M AND XS AND
CORTEN STEEL FOR S —
THUS ADDING TO THEIR
INDIVIDUAL CHARACTERS

THE BIG DIG HOUSE WEARS
ITS SALVAGED URBAN
INFRASTRUCTURE WITH
PRIDE: PARTS OF THE
HOUSE STARTED LIFE IN
BOSTON'S INFAMOUS
INTERSTATE 93 FLYOVER

Suburban | BIG DIG HOUSE
Single Speed Design
USA

Single Speed Design adopted a different definition of functionalism when it came to the Big Dig House in 2006. An exercise in creative recycling, this single-family house in Lexington, Massachusetts, was created around industrial and architectural waste products from Boston's 'Big Dig', the multi-billion-dollar project to re-route the city's major traffic arteries beneath the city to undo the legacy of post-war town planning.

One of the major criticisms of the Big Dig project was its colossal expense. The project involved the removal of a large section of elevated highway, which had to be retained and moved throughout the works. Enormous quantities of construction material, primarily steel and concrete, were slated to be discarded, a total of hundreds of thousands of tonnes of waste.

Single Speed Design, a studio founded by Jinhee Park and John Hong, takes sustainability as its core value, an approach that 'is inherently based on finding solutions that minimize material and energy use while maximizing performance'. The studio's Big Dig House demonstrated how waste materials, of all types and quality, can form the basis of innovative, low-impact architecture. The house was designed in conjunction with the client, Paul Pedini, a civil engineer working on the Boston infrastructure project. Pedini saw the potential of the materials he was being asked to remove, enabling 270,000 kilos (600,000 pounds) of waste to be diverted from landfill to this verdant site.

From the recycled aggregate that forms the foundation walls, through to the large-span steel trusses that are reused as a tough, muscular external structural system, the house is a prosaic reworking of the classic American tract home, viewed first through the prism of mid-century Modernism, then re-imagined in the light of the materials that were available. The core recycled element is the structural system, with the weathered and frayed steel and concrete sections of Interstate 93 being translated from off-ramp into floors and roofs. The time and cost savings made the budget around 25 per cent cheaper than a comparable 'new build', although this was largely due to the client's privileged access to a treasure trove of materials.

The Big Dig House is necessarily tough and industrial. The highway-grade steel and slab is over-scaled for the domestic environment, but creates a certain monumentality, certainly in the generous, double-height interiors, where the polished concrete floors set off exposed I-beams and industrial-grade balustrades and stairs. The huge steels form the core, supporting floor slabs linked by off-the-shelf components. Large expanses of flat roof provide ample space for roof gardens, while the industrial origin is domesticated by the wooden cladding and slat screens.

The design is intended to minimize energy consumption, thanks to the use of rainwater harvesting, solid thermal mass and efficient floor heating. The result is a structure that transcends its industrial origins, although it retains a certain nostalgic memory of the relentless urban highway marching above urban districts on vast steel piers. The architects are not interested only in residential recycling, preferring to think on a far larger scale and envisaging new community buildings benefiting from the constant flow of raw materials generated by major infrastructure projects.

Suburban | BIG DIG HOUSE
Single Speed Design
USA

01
BRINGING THE SALVAGED
COMPONENTS TO SITE.
A PRECAST CONCRETE
FOUNDATION AND STEEL
FRAME WERE RAPIDLY
TRANSFORMED INTO THE
SHELL OF THE HOME
WITH THE ADDITION OF
THESE VAST CONCRETE
FLOOR SLABS

02
SINGLE SPEED DESIGN
HAVE EXTRAPOLATED THE
SALVAGED COMPONENTS TO
CREATE A SPECULATIVE
BUILDING SYSTEM,
TURNING HIGHWAYS INTO
HOUSING AND SCHOOLS

03
THE VARIOUS ELEMENTS
OF THE BIG DIG HOUSE
REVEALED, BOTH
CONSTRUCTION PROCESS
AND AESTHETIC
UNDERPINNED BY
AVAILABLE MATERIALS

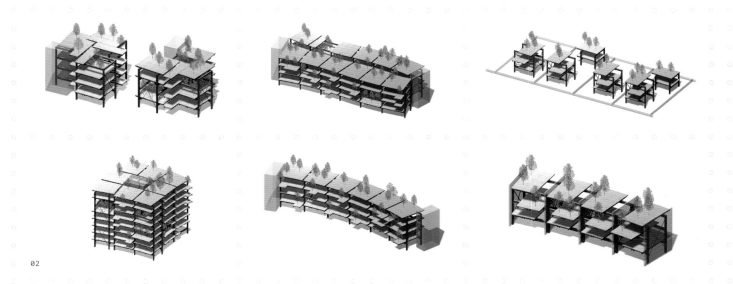

02

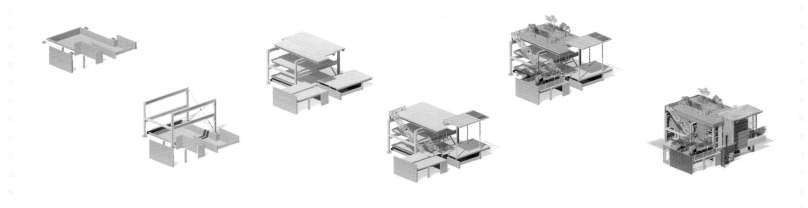

03

Suburban | ONE WINDOW HOUSE
Touraine + Richmond Architects
USA

Located in a small corner plot in Venice, Los Angeles, in the heart of the city's ever-changing urban landscape, the One Window House (2005) is an award-winning solution to the problems of high-density building, while also maintaining high standards in sustainability.

The architects Olivier Touraine and Deborah Richmond began designing a family house for themselves in an area popular with young creative professionals, at a time of sudden increase in property values. The economic conditions resulted in a sudden increase in residential additions and extensions to existing properties by many of the area's homeowners. Touraine and Richmond had a variety of different priorities and needs to satisfy, including their growing family, the house's resale value, and of course, the house as a representation of their own architectural manifesto.

The flat plot contained an existing dwelling from the early 1950s and an old native California alder tree. The architects worked with the target of creating a two-bedroom house, including a loft and three bathrooms. The Venice Specific Plan parking requirements were also an important factor, and to satisfy them, the team opted for a 'duplex' form; this would include two almost separate buildings, which could easily be converted to a single one, with flexible options for usage, for both working and living. This also allowed them five parking spaces on various locations in the plot.

A conscious contrast was developed between the Loos-inspired upper private rooms with the open-plan Corbusian ground level, where the house's public areas were located. Envisaged as a reflection of Los Angeles' often very polarized extremes of life and culture – a public side is reflected in the almost open ground floor and a very private one is seen in the upper level – this division was enhanced by the large aluminium-framed window openings on the ground floor, as opposed to the single window on the higher storeys that gives the house its name.

As far as materials were concerned, the architects' response was straightforward and function-based: 'craft was valued over preciousness of materials'. The exterior is clad in corrugated and galvanized metal, cellular polycarbonate, glass and plywood panels, while the main materials used inside were diamond-polished concrete, plastics and sanded OSB.

Sustainability was a primary concern. The combined steel- and wood-frame structure needed virtually no special heating and cooling plan: the area's microclimate allows temperature to be self-regulated via insulation, shaded glazing and the one upper window. Only native Californian plants were used in the garden, to limit the need for watering, while the primary building materials – such as the OSB – were made from recycled scraps.

In creating a low-environmental-impact house in a high-density urban area while also coordinating the privacy and functional needs of a family home, Touraine and Richmond offer a refreshing solution to Los Angeles' housing challenges.

LEFT
ONE WINDOW HOUSE TAKES ITS NAME FROM THE SINGLE WINDOW ON THE STRUCTURE'S UPPER FLOOR

ABOVE
AT GROUND LEVEL, INTERIOR AND EXTERIOR MIX, SEPARATED ONLY BY GLASS WALL AND DOORS

Urban

Urban | CASAS LAGO
Adamo-Faiden
Argentina

The Casas Lago are located in Floresta, a district in the western reaches of Buenos Aires' vast urban sprawl, a dense network of gridded streets that grew during the last years of the 19th century. Here, architects Sebastián Adamo and Marcelo Faiden, together with Carolina Leveroni, Paula Müller and Luciana Baiocco, have assembled a modest interpretation of the grand town house, retaining the proportions and dimensions of a traditional structure, yet cast with relatively humble industrial materials.

The Casas Lago (2007) make a virtue of lightness, with a double-skinned façade that sets back the windows behind a fine-meshed metal screen, allowing the apartments to stay secure and benefit from natural ventilation. The metal panels are overlaid on a concrete frame, with slender mullions rising up through the first and second floors before angling back in imitation of a mansard roof. Concrete walls are finished in green mosaic, giving the house a soft, organic palette of blues, greys and greens.

Built for the Lago family, the building contains two separate houses, their individual identities subsumed by the rigour of the façade. This was Adamo-Faiden's first major work, and demonstrates an approach driven by a modest manifesto. By making an enquiring statement that questions the role of the architect, builder and culture-maker in modern society, Adamo-Faiden are consciously associating with architects who have historically been happier committing their approach and world view to paper, rather than to bricks and mortar.

A subsequent project, the Edificio Conesa, contains three offices and nine apartments, wrapped up in a corrugated steel façade and steel mesh. Exposed concrete ceilings, stairs and floors are tempered by modest planting in the internal circulation courtyard. There are few soft edges in this building; it is a structure designed for functional habitation, a shell into which businesses and families will be poured.

The architects describe themselves as 'contemporary constructors', an almost metaphysical role that 'understands the world as a collection of particular facts in constant motion'. This idea of a world in flux – a 'mosaic without glue' – drives their architectural approach, acknowledging instability, uncertainty and subjectivity in all things, but also the constant presence and memory of recent history.

The influence of the everyday aesthetic shines through, in the choice of materials, the reductivist details and the architects' stated ideal of creating 'simple environments that allow multiple appropriations, letting inhabitants and everyday objects fit naturally'. Just as the Brutalist movement forced a visual reappraisal of the humble mass-produced object, so Sebastián Adamo and Marcelo Faiden seek to parcel up the many facets of modern life into their work, making each project a careful construction of historical and lived experience.

In practice, this blurring of a theoretical dissection of the world of objects with real, concrete practice loses some of the nuances of a manifesto-led approach, yet in an era of image-led architecture, Adamo and Faiden resist the temptation simply to shout louder than everyone else.

Urban | CUBICAL HOUSE
Boyd Cody
Ireland

Dermot Boyd and Peter Cody began their architectural collaboration in 1997, founding Boyd Cody in Dublin in 2000. Their work is thoughtful and mannered, occupying perhaps the same territory as Dominic Stevens (see p. 50) in their determination to eke out new ways of adapting and evolving existing systems. Here, the architects are exploring the backlands site, as part of the slow recolonization of lengthy urban gardens with modest new dwellings, densely arranged and self-contained, of the moment and without recourse to contextual pastiche.

This house in Alma Road, the Cubical House (2005), is awash with light. Bound by a tight site, the accommodation arrangements are inverted, with bedrooms at ground-floor level and living spaces above. A generous entrance hall in the centre of the plan acts as a division between the two ground-floor double bedrooms, along with a utility area. On the floor above,

a large living/dining area runs the full length of the plan, with two large windows sited so as to avoid being overlooked. A small kitchen opens off this space, while a conservatory – with glazed roof – brings light down the stairwell.

The house is built of load-bearing brick. The generous windows are free of mullions and lined in satin anodized aluminium, enhancing their role of frame when looked through from the inside. Iroko wood floors, doors and joinery are offset by white-plastered walls, creating a neutral space washed with natural light that will be the setting, eventually, for the client's life (decanting from the large Victorian house, the garden of which forms the site of the Cubical House).

Stating that 'we have the advantage, unlike other professions, in creating a tactile object or a sensual place', Boyd Cody believe strongly in the importance of creating a physical space; architecture is not a virtual

or a paper activity. 'Architecture should be truthful in its expression of structure, material and function,' they write, stating that a dualistic view of the world, drawn from philosophical discourse, can equally be applied to architecture, divided between 'the physical and the metaphysical; the knowable and unknowable or as [Louis] Kahn puts it, the measurable and immeasurable'.

Boyd Cody's work addresses functionalism at its most basic level; spaces that come alive through construction and occupation, employing a 'modesty of form and line, use of material, intervention, statement'. Mood – that unknowable, indefinable quality – is considered as important as form, with a limited materials palette deliberately being used to create a 'neutral backdrop' to everyday life.

THIS PAGE
THE HOUSE IS A
COMPOSITION OF BRICK,
WOOD AND PLASTER.
WINDOWS DOMINATE
THE FLAT FAÇADES,
EXPRESSING ROOM
POSITIONS AND ARRANGED
TO PROVIDE VIEWS OVER
THE SURROUNDINGS

OPPOSITE
THE FIRST-FLOOR LIVING
AREA: OPENINGS AND
DOORS ARE FULL-HEIGHT,
MAXIMIZING THE SENSE
OF SPACE. THE HOUSE
ACTS AS A FRAME
FOR ITS SURROUNDINGS

Urban | CUBICAL HOUSE
Boyd Cody
Ireland

02

03

04

01

01–04
SEQUENCE OF
CONSTRUCTION
PHOTOGRAPHS. THE
CUBICAL HOUSE WAS
BUILT IN AN EXISTING
BACK GARDEN

05
THE ORIGINAL CONCEPT
SKETCH, TO WHICH THE
FINISHED HOUSE IS
REMARKABLY FAITHFUL

05

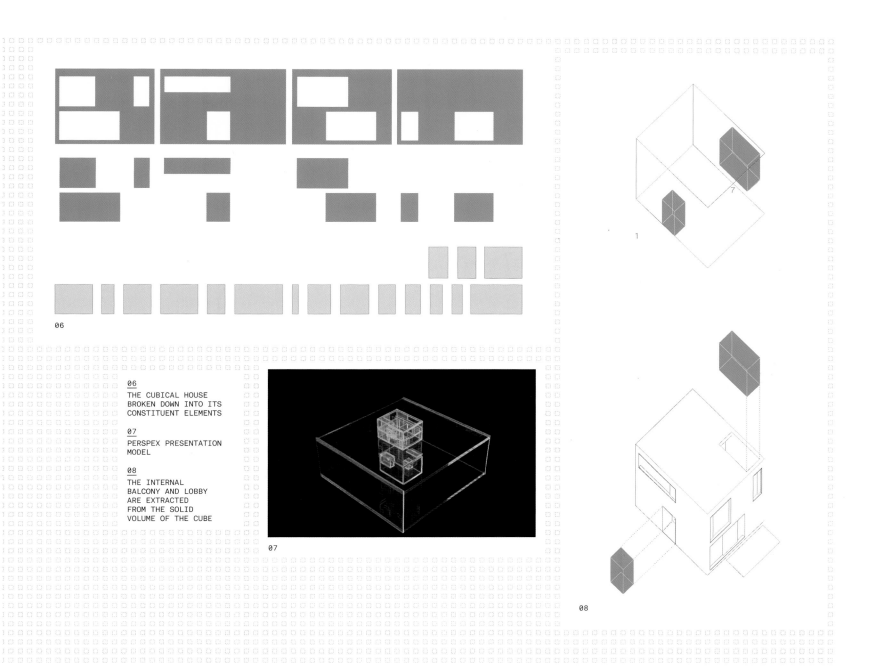

06

06
THE CUBICAL HOUSE
BROKEN DOWN INTO ITS
CONSTITUENT ELEMENTS

07
PERSPEX PRESENTATION
MODEL

08
THE INTERNAL
BALCONY AND LOBBY
ARE EXTRACTED
FROM THE SOLID
VOLUME OF THE CUBE

07

1

7

08

THIS PAGE
BEHIND THE WALL, A SERIES
OF COURTYARDS, TERRACES
AND STEPPED LEVELS CREATE
A PRIVATE DOMESTIC REALM

OPPOSITE
THE TWO HOUSES ARE SET
BEHIND A NEW WALL, THE
GREEN ROOF VISIBLE ABOVE
BUT ALL OTHER INDICATIONS
OF CONVENTIONAL
DOMESTICITY ABSENT

This pair of courtyard houses in the Liberties, a district in inner Dublin, was constructed on the site of a long-demolished church outbuilding in 2005. The land was subsequently abandoned and forgotten, lost behind the rather blank, pebble-dashed churchyard wall. The architect's strategy was to preserve the massing of the original streetscape by excavating the land, digging down to form two courtyard houses hidden behind a new wall.

The architect describes the houses, known as 0 and -1 John Dillon Street, as being a modern interpretation of the two-up two-down typology – 'the ubiquitous building type of Victorian Dublin'. In both plan form and spatial arrangement, the new houses evoke the original closely packed layout of worker's terrace housing, translating the rear yard into an internal courtyard in order to bring light down to the new ground floor, set 1.35 metres (4 feet 5 inches) beneath street level.

From within, each house is a complex series of inside and outside spaces, with views arranged across, through and down the site. With no external views, the houses draw all daylight through the courtyards and rooflights. The main living spaces are placed on the ground-floor level, with a kitchen and dining/sitting area overlooking a floor-to-ceiling glazing and a planted courtyard beyond. A metal-mesh staircase leads up to a communal roof terrace, surrounded by a shallow wall and featuring the 1834 church of St Nicholas of Myra as a backdrop. On the lower floor, two bedrooms are joined by a pair of baths, one internal, one external.

The houses use a simple material palette, including walls of exposed, shot-blasted concrete. All the hardwood used in the house is recycled. Finely wrought wooden staircases and tables are suspended from the ceilings, and one bed platform has been hinged in order to fold over as a desk for a home office; the houses are modestly sized, at around 93 square metres (1000 square feet), and clever planning such as this maximizes the internal space. Heating is placed underfloor and a universal glazing system in black anodized aluminium serves also as a conduit for the electrical services. Polished Carrara marble is used as flooring throughout, its highly reflective surface helping to diffuse the light around each house.

Tom de Paor cites Critical Regionalism as a key influence on his work – which merges architecture and art – as opposed to the 'cheaper and easier' path of straight Modernism. Critical Regionalism seeks to be a strategy for humanizing modern architecture via a more deliberate and considered approach to context, through the careful use of light and materials and with an emphasis on tactile rather than purely visual qualities. The John Dillon Street houses belong in this new tradition of contextual experimentation.

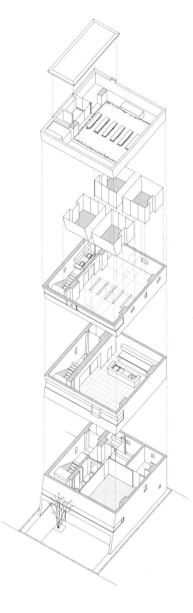

<u>LEFT</u>
K HOUSE TOOK ITS NAME
FROM THE 'K' SHAPE OF
THE EXTERNAL VOLUME

<u>ABOVE</u>
EXPLODED AXONOMETRIC
SHOWING THE HOUSE'S
DIFFERENT LEVELS

<u>OPPOSITE</u>
HIGH HORIZONTAL SLITS ON
THE MAIN FAÇADE PROVIDE
LIGHT FOR THE INTERIOR
WHILE ALSO REGULATING
THE OWNER'S CONTACT WITH
THE OUTSIDE

Urban | K HOUSE
Furumoto Architect Associates Co. Ltd
Japan

Hiroshima-based architect Ryuichi
Furumoto is familiar with the challenges of designing
for the dense urban landscape of the contemporary
Japanese city; having built some 20 new houses in the
last six years alone, he has dealt extensively with the
issues of residential design in both inner-city and rural
contexts. For this project, built in 2008, the clients
needed living and sleeping areas, as well storage and
extra spaces for the children to play. Additionally, given
that the project is set in downtown Hiroshima, the
planning requirements outlined stringent health and
environmental considerations, including the control
of sunlight, ambient noise and vibrations.

The commission came from a family of six – a couple
and their four children. With only a small site for the
house, Furumoto decided to work vertically, prioritizing
functionality. The result was a five-storey structure
(including the rooftop terrace level) with a minimal
floorplate, dubbed K House after the structure's actual
shape; the inward kink on the main tall façade's surface
appears to form a giant letter K. This device allows the
house to take a step back from the busy street to avoid
unnecessary exposure to the traffic. The curved façade
also provides the right conditions for sunlight

reflections, allowing daylight into the interior without
the need for overly large openings towards the street.
Narrow horizontal gaps on the slanted façade's surface
also bring natural light into the building.

By enclosing a simple yet multilayered interior space
within such a strong structure – in both shape and
material – Furumoto has provided the family with a
psychological and physical refuge from the city. By
shutting out its hustle and bustle, the architect has
achieved a sense of interior calm, enhanced by simple
gestures and the use of basic materials – exposed
concrete inside and out, with porcelain tiles, solid wood
flooring and extra wood panel finishing in the interior.

The client's initial brief called for a comfortable,
safe family home, so the interior layout was planned to
allow the family members to feel each other's presence.
While each level's ceiling height is different, the staircase
connecting all the floors acts as a large void within the
building's volume, spreading across all levels and uniting
them in a continuous space. The central role of the
staircase also facilitates circulation through the house.
Furthermore, this way light and air travels freely through
the house, making natural ventilation and lighting easier
and the structure more energy-efficient. This is not the

only green feature of the house; the building can be
fitted with solar energy-generating equipment, like
photovoltaic panels, and has an accessible planted roof,
which not only helps with insulation but offers a green
escape for the owners.

Furumoto's choice of material was deliberate and
carefully planned. He accepted the material palette's
importance in the design concept, and embraced the
qualities of concrete, wood and porcelain, choosing
them not just for durability and ease of maintenance,
but also according to the role he planned for them in
the final design. 'I do not agree with the concept that
materials are important in and of themselves,' he
explains; 'materials have value only after they interact
together with the beauty of their surroundings.'

Cleverly making the most out of the site's existing
urban condition and the innate qualities of the raw
materials, K House is a balanced design, true to its
brief and context, providing a model of functionality
and sustainability.

Urban | K HOUSE
Furumoto Architect Associates Co. Ltd
Japan

01

02

03

04

05

06

07

01-07
THE ARCHITECT'S STUDY
OF DIFFERENT TEXTURES
AND MATERIALS INFORMED
THE FINAL CHOICE OF
SHAPES AND MATERIALS

08-10
RUSSIAN DOLL-STYLE
BENTO BOXES ALSO
INSPIRED THE ARCHITECT
IN HIS ATTITUDE TOWARDS
THE INTERIOR LAYOUT
OF SPACES

08

09

10

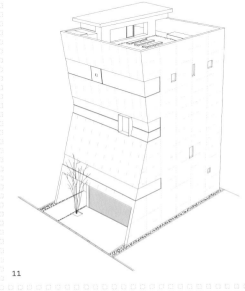

11

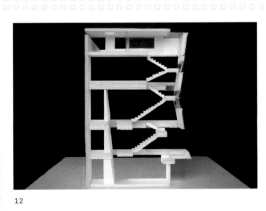

12

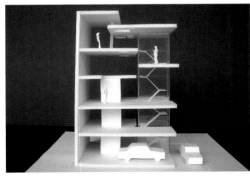

13

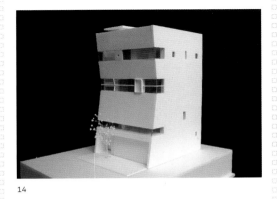

14

11
K HOUSE THREE-
DIMENSIONAL DRAWING

12-14
THREE DIFFERENT MODELS
OF THE HOUSE: THE
STAIRCASE CONNECTING
ALL LEVELS; AN
OPEN-SECTION MODEL
SHOWING THE INTERIOR;
AND THE FINAL MODEL

Urban | THE SBM
Christoph Seyferth
The Netherlands

Built for his own use as a house and work studio in the city of Maastricht in 2005, the SBM (Seyferth Building Maastricht) was designed by Dutch-based German-born designer and artist Christoph Seyferth. Finished in 2005, the project required a lengthy planning process and took more than six years to complete, but the end result truly represents the designer's vision. 'Nowadays, design only appears to be a game of codes, almost comparable with art,' says the designer, who has a training in fine art. 'If craftsmanship or manual work are of any importance, they are primarily used to create seductive images.'

The simple rectangular building may be located in an urban environment, but it is inspired by rural wooden houses, barns and farmers' sheds, all images drawn from the owner's own childhood. Seyferth was involved in every step of the process, from the seven-year-long planning procedure to the design and construction.

The house's down-to-earth exterior appearance is supported by an effortless and functional interior, featuring open-plan spaces, simple material (mainly clean concrete and wood) and large windows. The 380 square metre (4090 square foot) space is big enough to host not only Seyferth's work and living areas, but also two independent apartments on the upper two floors – meaning that part of it can be rented out when necessary, to support the owner's own business.

Choosing wood as the main material, Seyferth used rough-hewn vertical oak cladding for the exterior, enveloping the structure in a warm natural skin, which will age beautifully. The cladding is supported by a main concrete structural frame, the whole scheme being designed in collaboration with Amsterdam-based Dam & Partners Architects. And when all the windows are closed, using wooden shutters of the same material, the structure turns into a mystery-box, as the uniform façades leave no way of telling what lies within.

These games do not detract from the building's overall utilitarian approach. After all, functionality and its inseparable relationship with the beauty of the everyday is something Seyferth considers to be an inherent element of his work ethos: 'I believe in a kind of design in which the commissioner and the user are both important and the concept of function plays a leading part. I also see our daily use of things, our intimate relationship with objects, as a necessary condition for the experience of beauty.'

01

02

03

04

05

06

07

08

09

01-03
SEYFERTH'S INSPIRATION
VARIES IN ORIGIN, FROM
STRUCTURES ON VENICE'S
GRAND CANAL, TO OAK
TREES AND TRADITIONAL
WOODEN STOOLS

04-09
DIFFERENT STAGES OF
THE SBM'S CONSTRUCTION

10-11
THREE-DIMENSIONAL
DIGITAL MODELS
OF THE HOUSE, WITH
THE WINDOWS OPEN
AND CLOSED

12
THE FINAL RESULT, THE
SBM, CAN BE PARTLY
OPEN OR FULLY SHUT

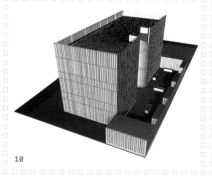

10

11

12

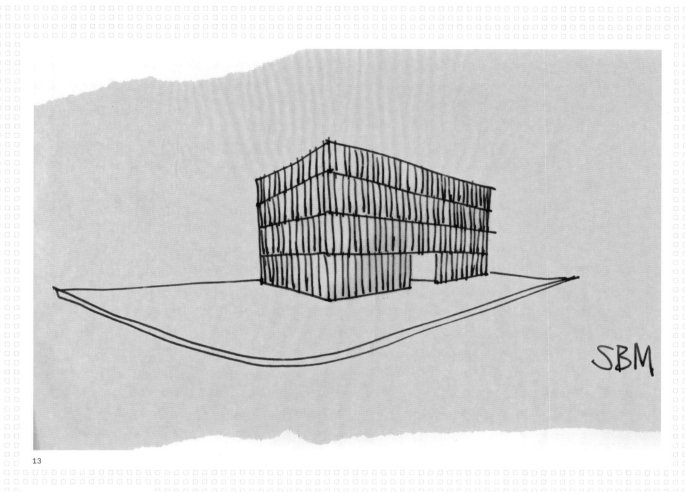

13

13
SEYFERTH'S SKETCH FOR
THE SBM ENCAPSULATES
THE VOLUME'S SIMPLICITY

A communal architecture born out of the spirit of anarchy, Brendeland & Kristoffersen Arkitekter's apartment building in Trondheim began life as a squat. Located in the town's run-down Svartlamoen district, the long-standing squat eventually attracted the creative classes, encouraging the city authorities to involve the building's occupants in the area's regeneration.

The Strandveien 37 building is actually two structures, built in 2006 to serve a newly established housing foundation. The two separate blocks, one of two and one of five storeys, include studio flats and communal apartments, with the ground-floor units given over to retail. The architects intended the structure to be low-cost, sustainable and at the same time entirely contemporary, addressing these key issues while also creating a soaring wood-clad form that would establish itself as a new focal point for the district.

Clad in a variety of slow-growing local pine that needs no weatherproofing and eventually fades and matures as the surface ages, the apartments are planned to stay true to the cooperative ideal, with 22 small private bedrooms in the low-level building offset by large, shared public spaces such as kitchens and meeting rooms. The rear is more ad hoc, with a tight courtyard arranged around an existing low-rise structure housing studios and living space, creating the kind of evolutionary, unplanned urban space that eludes rigorous town planning. The tougher front façade of the five-storey building faces on to a road, a rail line and a large industrial structure, and the steep mansard – which appears as a sharp kink in the wood façade – contains the studio apartments.

All circulation is external, via a large cantilevered steel staircase. The high-density project – about 22 square metres (240 square feet) per person – was built from large untreated timber components, assembled on-site in only a few days. The interiors are rough and monastic, and can be customized according to each inhabitant's furnishings and needs.

The sharp, prism-shaped building's sustainable credentials are not limited to the type of timber used; the outer walls are insulated with an additional layer of 200 millimetre (7.8 inch) mineral-wall gypsum boards. The window frames were also specially designed for minimum energy loss. The taller building was one of the first to use this particular timber system, demonstrating that wooden buildings can meet contemporary design standards, and also creating a sense of continuity within the tradition of Norwegian timber-built architecture.

Since completion, the architects have also undertaken the conversion of a nearby car showroom into a nursery, extending their notion of architecture as integral to community regeneration.

THIS PAGE
THE TRONDHEIM APARTMENT
BUILDING IS CLAD INSIDE
AND OUT IN VARIETIES OF
LOCAL PINE

OPPOSITE
THE WARM WOODEN INTERIORS
WERE DELIBERATELY KEPT
SIMPLE, SO THEY CAN ADAPT
TO EACH INHABITANT'S
INDIVIDUAL NEEDS

Urban | TRONDHEIM APARTMENT BUILDING
Brendeland & Kristoffersen Arkitekter
Norway

01

02

03

04

05

06

07

01-04
DIFFERENT STAGES
IN THE BUILDING'S
CONSTRUCTION, AS THE
PREFABRICATED ELEMENTS
ARRIVED AND WERE
ASSEMBLED ON SITE

05
SKETCH SHOWING LIFE
IN THE APARTMENT
BUILDING AS ENVISIONED
BY THE ARCHITECTS

06
MODEL OF THE STRUCTURE
STRIPPED OF THE
EXTERIOR WALLS IN
ORDER TO SHOW THE
BUILDING'S DIFFERENT
LEVELS

07
AERIAL VIEW OF THE
APARTMENT BUILDING
WITHIN ITS
SURROUNDINGS, SHOWING
IT CLEARLY STANDING
OUT IN AN AREA OF
MORE CONVENTIONAL
RESIDENCES AND
INDUSTRIAL BUILDINGS

Urban | BRICK HOUSE
Caruso St John
UK

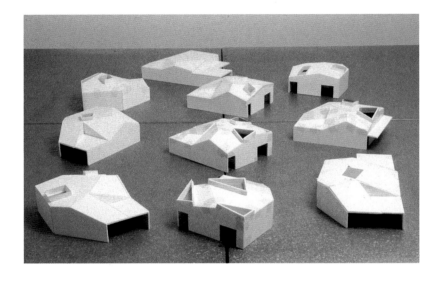

Central London's space and housing problems are well known even outside the UK, and the conditions in which the Brick House (2005) was created are the perfect illustration of this issue. The design, by East London-based architects Caruso St John, offered a particularly inventive and refreshing solution to the issue of urban infill, creating a house that functions as both domestic space and hermetic retreat from the world.

The site, destined to accommodate a family house, was an unusual, almost trapezoid-shaped plot, nestled between three larger buildings. Access was available only via a passage through the façade of the adjacent Victorian terrace house. The design began in 2001 and the construction process took almost four years to complete. The end result was a striking demonstration of the owners' strong will and the architects' determination to make the most out of this challenging brief.

Spread across two levels and covering the entire plot, apart from a number of small openings kept as gardens, Brick House features airy loft-like rooms of irregular, unconventional geometry. While using, as its name suggests, standard London brick as the main material inside and out – including the floors – the most striking element of the house is the cast-concrete roof of the upper floor. The faceted, almost accidental shape, reaches down to envelop the living spaces, stretching and bending over rooms of different height, appearing remarkably supple and flexible.

Private rooms are tucked in towards the centre of the plot, while larger, more social areas, such as the broad living space and the impressive main entrance hall, are carefully positioned closer to the layout's edges.

Located in a busy part of London, the building and the site combine to provide the perfect solution for the family's need for tranquillity and detachment from nearby street life. From ground level, the house can be glimpsed only through openings between buildings and the surrounding houses' windows. Brick House has practically no conventional façades and required an especially careful planning process. It demonstrates a particular response to the capital's issues of space and site, one which offers both a working architectural solution as well as a place of serenity and escape.

ABOVE
SEVERAL WORKING MODELS
WERE CREATED BEFORE
A FINAL SOLUTION WAS
REACHED

OPPOSITE
ONE OF THE FEW EXTERIOR
VIEWS OF BRICK HOUSE,
PEEKING BETWEEN
NEIGHBOURING BUILDINGS

Lynch Architects are emboldened by the prospect of an architectural debate, which in itself suggests that writing about building is as important an element of the process as construction itself. This house in Greenwood Road, East London, was completed in 2006. Described by the architects as a 'new Georgian house', it was explicitly intended to reference the adjoining Georgian terrace without compromising its own form or material independence.

Semi-detached from its immediate neighbour, the house is anchored to the site by the sunken lower ground floor, a white brick structure that references the brick and rendered walls facing the road. Above this 'inhabited foundation' are two storeys constructed from timber, a 'bird's nest' perched on a 'sunken well'. From the tightly controlled daylight of the ground floor, rising up to a warmer light filtered through rooflights and bounced off the exposed oak frame, the house is an experiment in domestic landscape.

Material quality, craft and experience are crucial elements of Lynch Architects' work. Established by Patrick and Claudia Lynch, the studio is strongly rooted in the late-flowering period of expressive British Modernism, and the practice of writing about architecture as well as building. Everywhere in this modest house, concerns for material experience dominate, from the thin oak panels that line the landing ('like a cigar box') to the thick, muscular rhythm of the oak frame. The progression from enclosed basement to open upper floor brings the occupants out in the heart of the city, looking over rooftops and gardens.

For Lynch Architects, practice, culture and language are inseparable, bound by a combination of tradition and fact. Patrick Lynch has written that 'architecture is the articulation of mute matter, not just as metaphor, but as fact. Matter of fact qualities are such that wood will bend, concrete can be poured, glass is floated, bricks combine, steel is stiffened, stone is heavy but brittle, plastics thin but strong; and that materials can inspire form.' [1]

The Greenwood Road house expresses Lynch's belief that domestic architecture can form a harmonious and valuable whole, with a focus on typicality, on the familiar and the functional.

GREENWOOD ROAD IS A SEMI-DETACHED HOUSE THAT SLOTS INTO THE VICTORIAN STREETSCAPE. THE WOODEN-CLAD UPPER STOREYS SIT ABOVE A PAINTED BRICK BASE. THE HOUSE IS EARNEST AND QUOTIDIAN, WITH OCCASIONAL RICH DETAILS STANDING OUT FROM THE EVERYDAY SIMPLICITY OF THE CONSTRUCTION

1 | Patrick Lynch, 'Design as translation and typicality: on autonomy & contingency in architecture', Building Material (AAI), 2007

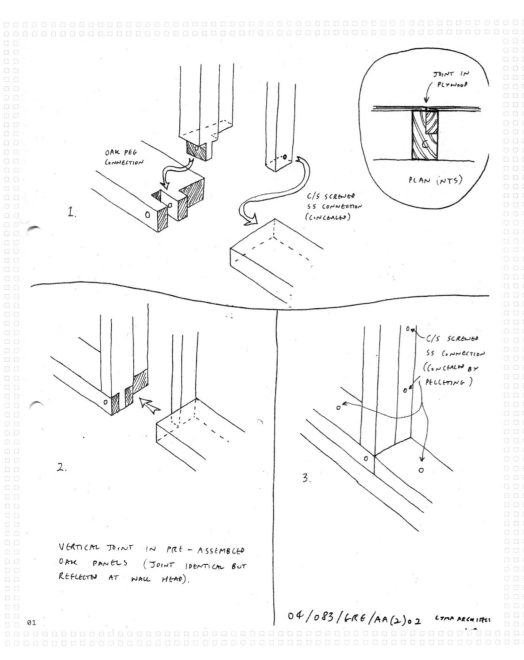

OAK PEG
CONNECTION

JOINT IN
PLYWOOD

PLAN (NTS)

1.

C/S SCREWED
SS CONNECTION
(CONCEALED)

2.

VERTICAL JOINT IN PRE-ASSEMBLED
OAK PANELS (JOINT IDENTICAL BUT
REFLECTED AT WALL HEAD).

C/S SCREWED
SS CONNECTION
(CONCEALED BY
PELLETING)

3.

C/S SCREWED
SS CONNECTION
(CONCEALED BY
PELLETING)

01

04/083/GRE/AA(2)02   LYNCH ARCHITECTS

02

01-02

THE HOUSE IS
CONSTRUCTED USING
TRADITIONAL WOOD-
WORKING TECHNIQUES:
AN OAK FRAME SECURED
WITH OAK PEGS, COMBINED
WITH PLYWOOD PANELS AND
PREFABRICATED ELEMENTS

03-04

DETAILED AXONOMETRIC
DRAWINGS OF THE WOODEN
FRAME

05

INITIAL CONCEPT SKETCH.
THE ARCHITECTS LIKEN
THE 'WOODEN BOX', WITH
ITS OAK-LINED INTERIOR,
TO A CIGAR BOX

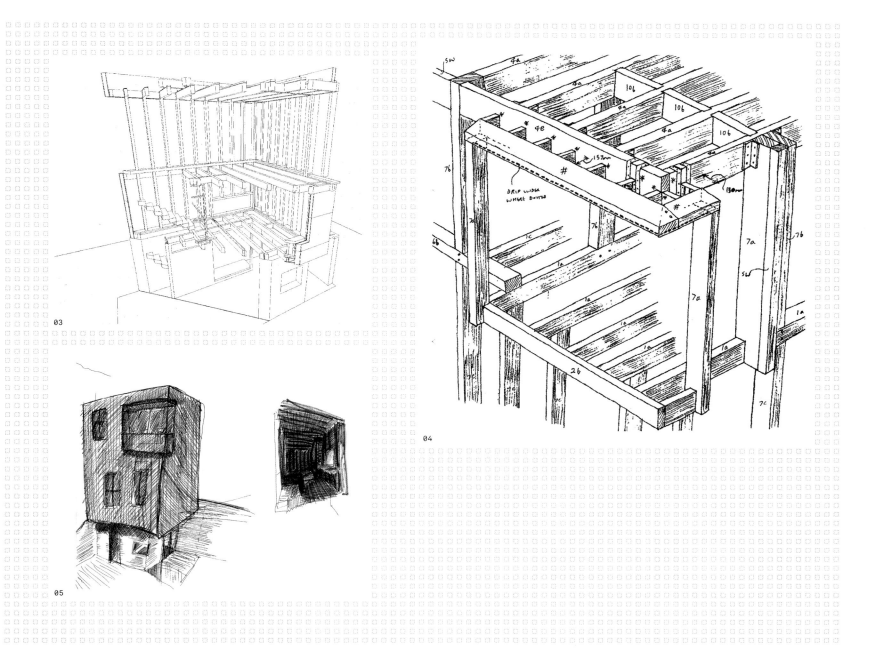

03

04

05

06

08

06-07
UNDER CONSTRUCTION:
THE WOODEN FRAME
IS INSTALLED. BELOW,
A DETAIL OF THE
WOOD PANELLING

08
THE EMPTY SITE BEFORE
CONSTRUCTION BEGAN: A
TYPICAL LONDON TERRACE

09-10
PRESENTATION MODELS
OF THE FINALIZED
DESIGN. THE HOUSE
IS PART-ATTACHED TO
THE EXISTING TERRACE
TO THE LEFT. THE
BRICK BASE IMPLIES
THE NEW STRUCTURE
HAS GROWN ORGANICALLY
ON THE SITE

07

09

10

11

12

<u>11–12</u>
THE FINISHED HOUSE
BEFORE OCCUPATION,
THE RICH CHARACTER OF
THE WOOD AND CAREFUL
JOINERY CREATING AN
ATMOSPHERIC SENSE
OF PLACE AND HUMAN
INVOLVEMENT

13

<u>13</u>
THE REAR FAÇADE. LESS
SELF-CONSCIOUS THAN
THE FRONT, LIKE THE
NEIGHBOURING HOUSES
THE REAR FEATURES LARGE
WINDOWS OVERLOOKING
THE GARDENS

14

<u>14</u>
SECTION. THE GROUND
FLOOR IS SET SLIGHTLY
BELOW GROUND LEVEL,
ALLOWING FOR THREE
STOREYS TO BE
ACCOMMODATED WITHIN
THE HOUSE WITHOUT
COMPROMISING
CEILING HEIGHTS

Urban | NEWINGTON GREEN HOUSE
Prewett Bizley Architects
UK

Flexibility and adaptability on all levels was one of the architects' main goals in the design of this residential project in North London. The house was built in 2005 on a tiny derelict site that used to be the adjoining Victorian terraced house's garden and subsequently the storage space for a nearby shop. It was destroyed by fire in 1999. Today it showcases an example of architectural inventiveness, with architect and client collaborating for the creative reuse of unconventional sites in a city much in need of space.

The client was also an architect. His requirement was for a building to act as both his house and his office space, as well as being adaptable to different possible future uses – from his growing family's increasing need for space, to the requirements of potential part-renting. Planning permission was granted in 2001 and work began immediately. The building covers nearly the whole of the site, apart from a narrow strip running parallel to the pavement. Build costs for the Newington Green House were a minimal amount for a building of its size. The project was completed in 2005.

The house was created to respond to its surroundings, with massing determined by the neighbouring buildings. For example, the upper floors had to be set back to allow light into adjacent houses, so the structure's context-sensitive character was reflected in nearly every room, affecting the overall orientation and openings. The spatial requirements were equally important; for economy of space, for example, the staircase was lined with bookshelves and treated as an extra room.

The architects worked closely on the relationship between the structure, the site and the locale. The grey bricks are a reference to the surrounding old Georgian and 1950s London houses, while the Douglas fir window frames give the building a more contemporary feel, with the larger ground floor windows connecting the house to the outside and the street, a link controlled with a combination of shutters and blinds.

The building's practical approach and efficiency are extended to high levels of sustainability – it utilizes passive climate-control systems, while the masonry walls and concrete ground slab give it a high thermal mass. Underfloor heating on the ground level helps air to circulate around all levels, providing passive ventilation.

Using simple and traditional materials and a low-cost, low-impact approach, Prewett Bizley created a richly textured house with a strong connection – both conceptual and visual – to its surroundings.

ABOVE
THE HOUSE'S GROUND-FLOOR
TOP-LIT KITCHEN AND
LIVING AREA

OPPOSITE
NEWINGTON GREEN HOUSE'S
IRREGULAR WINDOW
PLACEMENT RESULTS FROM
THE NEIGHBOURING
BUILDING'S MASSES AND THE
INTERNAL SPATIAL ECONOMY

01

02

03

04

05

11

06

07

08

09

10

01-05
FOR THE HOUSE,
THE ARCHITECTS DREW
INSPIRATION FROM
ISLINGTON'S 1950S
HOUSING [1,3,4,5],
AND FROM ARCHITECT SIR
JOHN SOANE'S WORK [2]

06-10
THE SITE WAS IN
A DERELICT STATE
WHEN WORKS FOR THE
HOUSE BEGAN

11
THE HOUSE'S
FINAL MODEL

12
SOME OF THE
ARCHITECTS' SKETCHED
DESIGNS FOR THE HOUSE

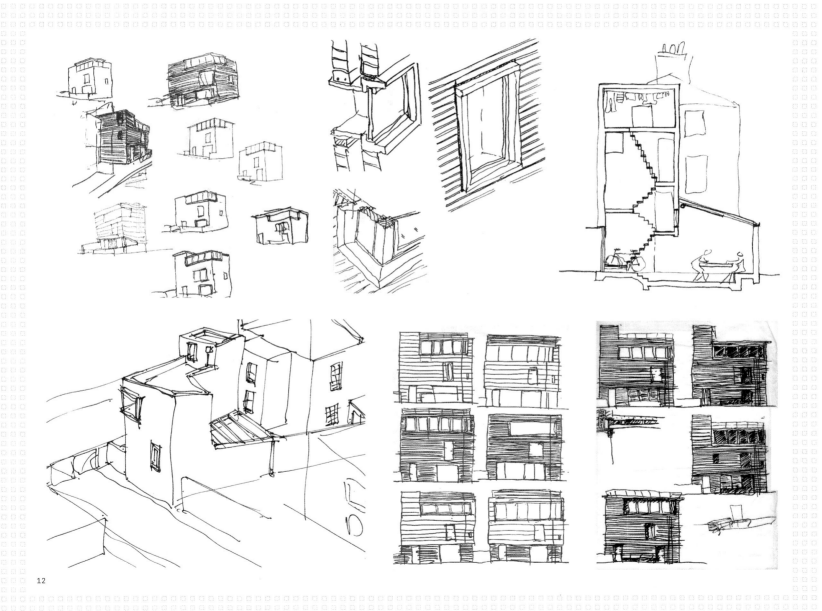

Urban | TWOFOLD HOUSE
Cassion Castle Architects
UK

Looking to build a house which would take them away from the city's noise and stress, a couple of industrial designers found a small and challenging site in East London's Bethnal Green area to create a home and workspace. Located in a semi-industrial alleyway formed by rows of old converted warehouses and running parallel to Bethnal Green Road, the project offered a complex problem for local architects Cassion Castle and Carl Turner, who won the commission in 2005.

The architects worked towards designing a space with minimum views out, prioritizing their clients' request for a house as sanctuary. The intention was to create an interior that was as calm, minimal and functional as possible. The entrance was kept deliberately simple, an elegant double-height glass box hanging over a recessed black-painted door, underlining their intention for discretion.

The structure, built in 2008, was designed as two interlocking L-shaped volumes, containing both home – on the upper levels – and workspace – on ground floor – each with an open-plan layout. The two parts communicate via an internal balcony in the bedroom area, overlooking the concrete floored double-height studio space, an area which also serves as a living room. To one side, the building is wedged up against an existing adjoining terrace, allowing for an extra study room to be created, slightly oversailing the neighbouring building.

The interior is painted a pure white to create a neutral and relaxing atmosphere. The bedroom, bathroom, kitchen and dining room, together with a joint living and studio area are spread across three levels. The light is filtered in through clerestory windows and a lightwell, while an upper-floor terrace offers uninterrupted views towards the nearby park.

Carving out spaces from a single block in order to make the most out of the site's small size, the architects also incorporated flexibility in the design. On a bright day the owners can open up the studio, folding back the dark entrance door to unite the residence's open plan, the work area and the alleyway into one single flowing space.

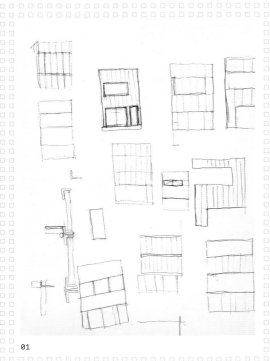

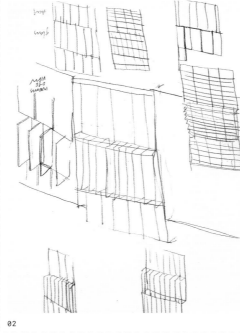

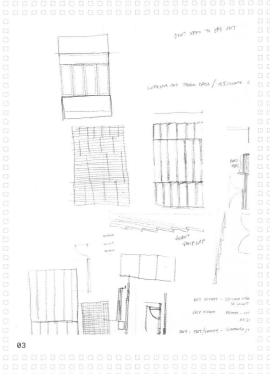

01

02

03

01–03
THE ARCHITECTS STUDIED
THE FAÇADE EXTENSIVELY:
ITS OPENINGS, DETAILING
AND GEOMETRIES

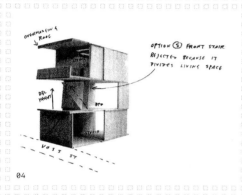

OPTION ③ FRONT STAIR
REJECTED BECAUSE IT
DIVIDES LIVING SPACE

04

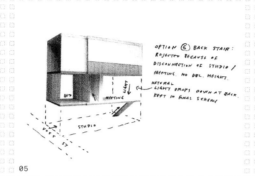

OPTION ⑥ BACK STAIR:
REJECTED BECAUSE OF
DISCONNECTION OF STUDIO /
MEETING. NO DBL. HEIGHT.

NATURAL
LIGHT DROPS DOWN AT BACK.
KEPT IN FINAL SCHEME.

05

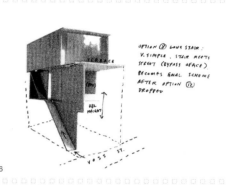

OPTION ⑧ LONG STAIR:
V. SIMPLE. STAIR MEETS
STREET (BYPASS OFFICE)
BECOMES FINAL SCHEME
AFTER OPTION ⑫
DROPPED

06

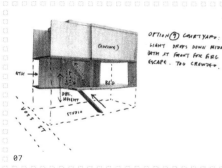

OPTION ⑨ COURTYARD:
LIGHT DROPS DOWN MIDDLE
BOTH AT FRONT FOR FIRE
ESCAPE. TOO CROWDED.

07

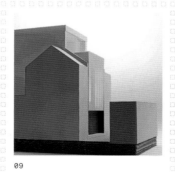

OPTION ⑫: MEZZANINE
FRONT RUNNER FOR A
LONG TIME. REJECTED
FOR BEING TOO BUSY.

PLATFORM ARTICULATED
AS 'BOX' WITHIN SPACE.

08

04–08
PRELIMINARY STUDIES
FOR THE INTERIOR
LAYOUT, INCLUDING
THE ARCHITECTS' NOTES

09–10
THE HOUSE'S FINAL
MODELS, SHOWING BOTH
EXTERIOR AND INTERIOR

09

10

Urban | SLOT HOUSE
noroof architects
USA

LEFT
THE STAIRCASE ALSO
ACTS AS A LIGHT WELL

OPPOSITE
THE SLOT CUT VERTICALLY
IN THE FRONT FAÇADE,
WHICH GIVES THE HOUSE
ITS NAME, LOOKS OUT
AT THE SINGLE TREE IN
THE FRONT YARD

'If *we had* to pick a primary author for the Slot House project, it would be the house itself,' say noroof principles Scot Oliver and Margarita McGrath. When the couple found themselves with a 90-year-old house in New York, intending to build their own home and studio on the plot, their primary concern was to establish a dynamic dialogue between the structure and the site itself. Certain that this would lead them to the best architectural solution for the project, the architects followed 'an unassuming approach to modernism and minimalism, reductive, not to diminish its scope, but to amplify it, bearing down on what is left'.

Oliver and McGrath put together their own manifesto-like brief for the house, including four main points; preserving the single existing tree on the plot; abolishing all fetishes towards materials and forms; the acceptance that modesty should be part of their design, not only because of their relatively small budget, but also because they personally preferred such an environment rather than over-designed sleek architecture; and finally, the engagement of memory in their design.

The architects began by deciding to retain the existing house and simply level the floors and add a new roof, saving the maple tree and also the opening that it created towards the road. A slot was cut in the front façade so that the owners can see the tree from inside the house. Inside, the architects continued to open up the building's structure, exposing the original cedar frame and handmade brick.

The idea of the slot worked so well that it quickly became the central concept of the design. The architects proceeded to cut additional slots, vertically and horizontally, in the house's façade and interior, extending the visual perception of the interior space by connecting different parts of the house in an open-plan loft-style space.

Treating the site and existing conditions pragmatically and taking decisions based on the structure's overall best functionality – regarding natural light, views, size and so on – the architects used basic building materials wherever possible, including concrete, metal grilles and meshes, cedar panels and birch veneer. Some elements have a double functional role: the central staircase works as a physical bridge between the different levels of the existing structure and also acts as a lightwell, while the metal grille on the back deck can also be used as a ladder. The house was completed in 2005.

By maintaining a human scale and working in harmony with the found condition, using modest materials, Oliver and McGrath have succeeded in enhancing the potential of both the site and the existing structure, creating a home that also epitomizes their practice's design approach and philosophy.

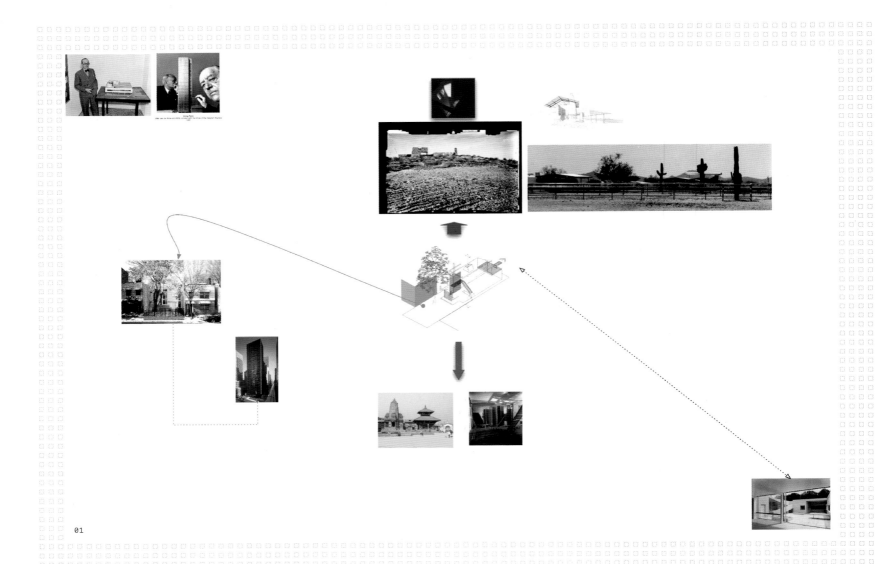

01

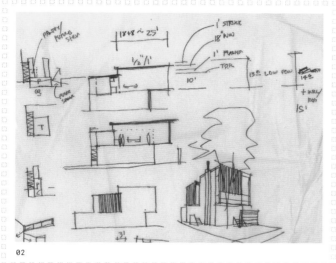

02

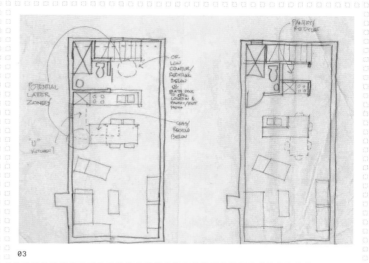

03

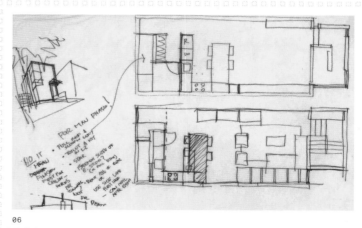

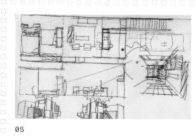

05

01

DIAGRAM TELLING THE
STORY OF THE SLOT
HOUSE'S INSPIRATION
SOURCES – FROM FRANK
LLOYD WRIGHT AND LE
CORBUSIER TO TRADITIONAL
ASIAN ARCHITECTURE AND
THE PLOT ITSELF WITH ITS
LONE MAPLE TREE

02-06

EARLY HAND DRAWINGS OF
THE HOUSE'S FLOOR PLANS,
SECTIONS AND ELEVATIONS

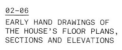

06

04

Urban | LIVE/WORK STUDIO IN PITTSBURGH
Studio D'Arc
USA

The urban studio is a contemporary genre with its roots in the emergence of the post-industrial era, as formerly commercial buildings were rescued from disuse and demolition by those with a desire for more living and working space. Subsequently, the functional live/work aesthetic spilled over into domestic design as architects and designers adopted rough finishes and industrial-grade fixtures and fittings in an attempt to impart the romance of ruin, reuse and patina to new-build projects.

The Live/Work Studio (2007) in Pittsburgh's South Side represents a hybrid architectural style, a quasi-industrialized façade and interior that adopts the proportions and dimensions of a traditional row-house, reflecting the mixed-use qualities of the neighbourhood. The site was a slot between two 19th-century houses, part of a terrace that was once a ubiquitous typology in this part of America, derived from European city housing but adapted for local conditions. Here there was scope to create an expansive private house and workplace slightly grander than the standard 'two-up, two-down' houses elsewhere in the city.

The ground floor incorporates a garage, entrance hall, and open-plan kitchen and living area, a fluid space that runs out into the small rear garden. The floor above houses the studio space and the master suite, separated by the upper part of the double-height kitchen below, a gap connected by a glass bridge. The top floor is given over to a roof terrace at the front and a green roof at the rear, with a remote-control skylight allowing light and, when required, fresh air, down into the living area.

The party walls are left as exposed concrete blocks, forming two grey cliffs, between which a landscape of complex and beautifully built maple joinery, floors and windows are inserted. The Live/Work Studio's two façades also evoke the residential and industrial nature of this part of town, with Corten steel, asphalt shingles and mahogany slats combining to create a tough, abstract statement that is far removed from the neat domesticity on either side. These materials are hard-wearing and low-maintenance.

Pittsburgh's urban qualities were the starting point for Studio D'Arc's design. A city 'once consumed with industry and construction ... [Pittsburgh] was once inspired by the natural resources of its place'. For this project, the architects wrote, they once again looked 'toward the region ... for clues on how to build within it. Materials and methods are selected for building performance, regional construction traditions, and regional material availability.'

This emerging form of pragmatism frequently runs counter to ingrained design and planning practices, wherein true vernacular forms and materials are often trumped by a dominant style – the honey colour of Bath stone, for example, deemed appropriate only in Georgian-style pastiche. Pittsburgh is not nearly as genteel as a West Country spa town. Built around a mighty steel industry, the city also produced glass and other building materials in its factories. The new house lies close to the historical industrial district, and these densely packed row-houses were once home to some of the city's hundreds of thousands of millworkers. The construction materials, from the Corten steel to the concrete blocks, reference the region's past; 'the house transforms from fragmentary to finished as one moves through the house from front to back.'

A form of neo-vernacular Critical Regionalism, the Live/Work Studio is reverential and low-key, an honest reflection of how changing times demand changing approaches to design.

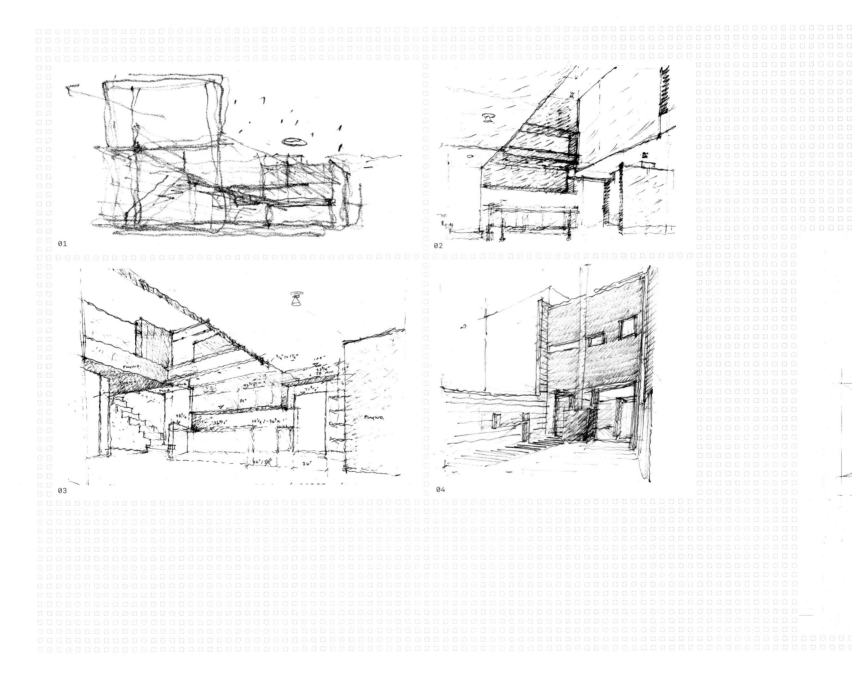

01

02

03

04

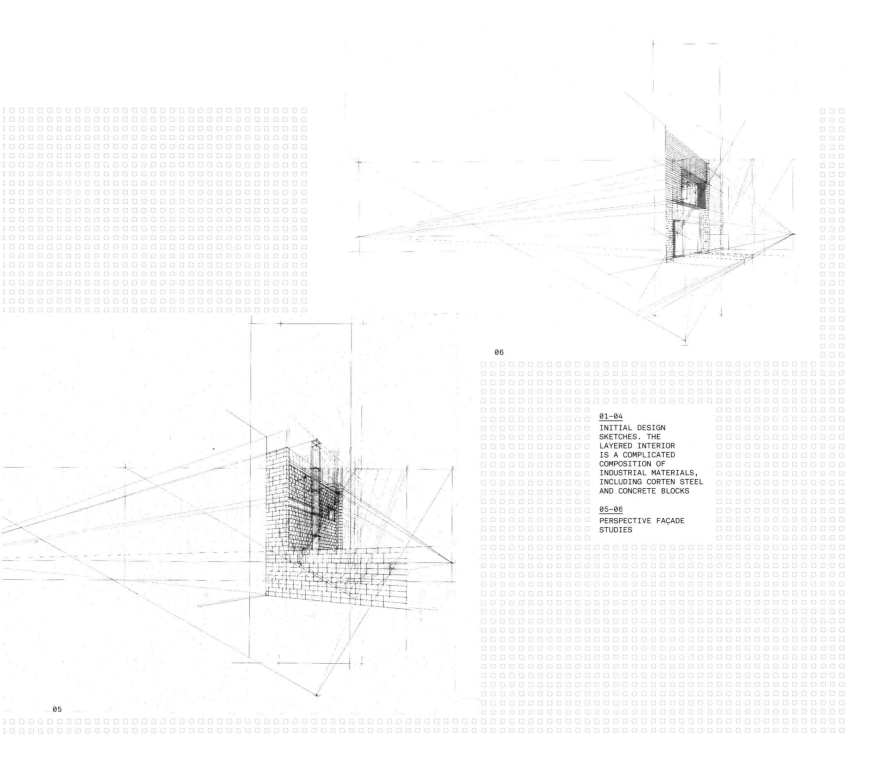

06

01-04
INITIAL DESIGN
SKETCHES. THE
LAYERED INTERIOR
IS A COMPLICATED
COMPOSITION OF
INDUSTRIAL MATERIALS,
INCLUDING CORTEN STEEL
AND CONCRETE BLOCKS

05-06
PERSPECTIVE FAÇADE
STUDIES

05

ARCHITECTS' CONTACTS

ARGENTINA
Adamo-Faiden
Florida 833
Oficina 334 (c1005aaq)
Buenos Aires
www.adamo-faiden.com.ar

AUSTRALIA
Casey Brown Architecture
Level 1, 63 William Street
East Sydney
NSW 2010
www.caseybrown.com.au

AUSTRIA
Popelka Poduschka Architekten (PPAG)
Gumpendorferstraße 65
1060 Wien
www.ppag.at

BELGIUM
Broekx-Schiepers Architects
Maastrichtersteenweg 60
3500 Hasselt
www.broekx-schiepers.be

BRAZIL
Andrade Morettin Arquitetos
rua Major Sertório 463 conj 22
São Paulo SP
www.andrademorettin.com.br

CHILE
Pezo von Ellrichshausen Architects
Lo Pequen 502, Concepcion
www.pezo.cl

CZECH REPUBLIC
Kamil Mrva Architects
Architektonické studio
Záhumenní 1358
742 21 Kopřivnice
www.mrva.net

FRANCE
Beckmann-N'Thépé
5, rue d'Hauteville
75010 Paris
www.b-nt.biz

Philippe Gazeau Architecte
21, rue de la Fontaine au Roi
75011 Paris
www.philippegazeau.com

Tank Architectes
7, rue du Chemin de fer
59100 Roubaix
www.tank.fr

Xavier Fouquet
5, rue Perrault
44000 Nantes

GERMANY
Thomas Bendel Architekt
Leuschnerdamm 41
10999 Berlin
www.thomasbendel.com

Titus Bernhard Architekten
Gögginger Straße 105a
D – 86199 Augsburg
www.titusbernhardarchitekten.com

IRELAND
Boyd Cody
36 College Green
Dublin 2
www.boydcodyarch.com

De Paor Architects
77 Merrion Square
Dublin 2
www.depaor.com

Dominic Stevens Architect
Cloone, Co. Leitrim
www.dominicstevensarchitect.net

JAPAN
Furumoto Architect Associates Co. Ltd
1-11 Hagoromo-cho Naka-ku
Hiroshima-city, Hiroshima 730-0814
www.furumotoaa.co.jp

Takao Shiotsuka Atelier
301-4-1-24, Miyako-machi,
Oita-shi, Oita 870-0034
www.shio-atl.com

LATVIA
ARHIS
Skarnu iela 4
LV 1050 Riga
www.arhis.lv

THE NETHERLANDS
Christoph Seyferth
Weustenraadstraat 3
6217 HZ Maastricht
www.seyferth.nl

SeARCH
Hamerstraat 3
1021 JT Amsterdam
www.search.nl

NORWAY
Brendeland & Kristoffersen Arkitekter
Fjordgata 50
7010 Trondheim
www.bkark.no

JVA
Hausmannsgate 6
0186 Oslo
www.jva.no

Rintala Eggertsson Architects
Stavangergata 46a
0467 Oslo
www.rintalaeggertsson.com

PORTUGAL
Álvaro Leite Siza Vieira
Rua do Aleixo, 53 – Cave A
4150 – 043 Porto
alvarinhosiza@sapo.pt

Atelier Central Arquitectos
Rua Ricardo Espirito Santo, 9
1200 – 790 Lisboa

Correia Ragazzi Arquitectos
Rua Azevedo Coutinho, 39 – 4ª sala 44
4100 – 100 Porto
www.correiaragazzi.com

SPAIN
Jesús Castillo Oli
www.jesuscastillooli.com

Juan Herreros Arquitectos
Calle Princesa 25
El Hexágono
28008 Madrid
www.herrerosarquitectos.com

SWEDEN
Strata Arkitektur / Petra Gipp Arkitektur AB
Klevgränd 16
SE 116 46 Stockholm
www.strataarkitektur.se
www.gipparkitektur.se

SWITZERLAND
Andreas Fuhrimann Gabrielle Hächler Architekten
Hardturmstrasse 66
8005 Zurich
www.afgh.ch

Degelo Architekten
St Jakobsstrasse 54
4052 Basel
www.degelo.net

EM2N Architekten
Josefstrasse 92
8005 Zurich
www.em2n.ch

Felix Jerusalem
Scharacher 7
8053 Zurich
www.strohhaus.net

Jomini Zimmermann Architects
Wasserwerkstrasse 129
8037 Zurich
www.j-z.ch

Thomas Jomini Architecture Workshop
Nordring 42
3013 Bern
www.thomasjomini.ch

Wespi de Meuron Architekten
6578 Caviano
www.wespidemeuron.ch

UNITED KINGDOM
BBM Sustainable Design
Star Brewery
Castle Ditch Lane
Lewes
East Sussex BN7 1YJ
www.bbm-architects.co.uk

Carl Turner Architects
Unit 2
Providence Yard
Ezra Street
London E2 7RJ
www.ct-architects.co.uk

Caruso St John Architects
1 Coate Street
London E2 9AG
www.carusostjohn.com

Cassion Castle Architects
Studio 5
51 Derbyshire Street
London E2 6JQ
www.cassioncastle.com

Charles Barclay Architects
74 Josephine Avenue
London SW2 2LA
www.cbarchitects.co.uk

Jonathan Tuckey Design
Unit 44
Pall Mall Deposit
124 Barlby Road
London W10 6BL
www.jonathantuckey.com

Lynch Architects
1 Amwell Street
London EC1R 1UL
www.lyncharchitects.co.uk

Prewett Bizley Architects
Unit 3M
Leroy House
436 Essex Road
London N1 3QP
www.prewettbizley.com

USA
noroof architects
134 Adelphi Street
Brooklyn, NY 11205
www.noroof.net

Paul Cha Architect
611 Broadway, Suite 540
New York, NY 10012
www.paulchaarchitect.com

Single Speed Design
325 West 38th Street, Suite 208
New York, NY 10018
171 Brookline Street
Cambridge, MA 02139
www.ssdarchitecture.com

Studio Atkinson Architecture
546 Guinda Street
Palo Alto, California
www.studioatkinson.com

Studio D'Arc
139 South 22nd Street
Pittsburgh, PA 15203
www.sdapgh.com

Touraine + Richmond Architects
2129 Linden Avenue
Venice, CA 90291
www.touraine-richmond.com

UNI Architects
15 Clifton Street
Cambridge, MA
www.uni-a.com

BIBLIOGRAPHY

The Architectural Review, December 1936

Bedell, Geraldine, 'The Young Generation with a New Vision to Build Britain', *The Observer,* 21 June 2009

Benton, Tim, *The Modernist Home*, V&A Publications, London, 2006

Borden, Iain, Joe Kerr, Jane Rendell and Alicia Pivaro (eds), *Unknown City: Contesting Architecture and Social Space*, MIT Press, Cambridge, Massachusetts, and London, 2002

Boudon, Philippe, *Lived-in Architecture: Le Corbusier's Pessac Revisited*, Lund Humphries, London, 1972

Cook, Peter, 'Let's be serious – let's be dogmatic', *The Architectural Review*, November 2008

Glancey, Jonathan, 'Whatever happened to craft?', *Building Design*, 27 March 2009

Gregory, Rob, 'Peter Zumthor' (interview), *The Architectural Review*, May 2009

Gropius, Walter, *The New Architecture and the Bauhaus*, Faber and Faber, London, 1935

Hatherley, Owen, 'Penthouse and Pavement', *The Guardian*, 2 May 2009

Jencks, Charles, *Critical Modernism*, Wiley Academy, London, 2007

Kolb, Jaffer and Patricio Mardones, 'Chile', *The Architectural Review*, June 2009

Lichtenstein, Claude and Thomas Schregenberger (eds), *As Found: The Discovery of the Ordinary*, Lars Müller Publishers, Baden, 2001

Neumann, Dietrich, 'Three Early Designs by Mies van der Rohe', *Perspecta: The Yale Architectural Journal*, vol. 27, 1992

Scott, Fred, *On Altering Architecture*, Routledge, London, 2008

Sullivan, Louis, 'The Tall Office Building Artistically Considered', *Lippincott's Magazine*, no. 57, March 1896

Till, Jeremy, *Architecture Depends*, MIT Press, Cambridge, Massachusetts, 2009

Van der Rohe, Mies, 'Bauen', *G2*, September 1923

Virilio, Paul, *Bunker Archaeology*, second edition, Princeton Architectural Press, New York, 2009

Wolfe, Tom, *From Bauhaus to Our House*, Farrar, Straus and Giroux, New York, 1981

Zumthor, Peter, *Atmospheres*, Birkhauser, Basel, 2006

FURTHER READING

Banham, Reyner, *A Critic Writes: Selected Essays*, University of California Press, Berkeley, 1996

Becher, Bernd and Hilla Becher, *Basic Forms of Industrial Buildings*, Schirmer/Moses, Munich, 2005

Caruso, Adam, *The Feeling of Things*, Ediciones Poligrafa, Barcelona, 2009

Frampton, Kenneth, *Modern Architecture: A Critical History*, Thames & Hudson, London, 2007

Harris, Steven and Deborah Berke (eds), *Architecture of the Everyday*, Princeton Architectural Press, New York, 1997

Le Corbusier, *Toward an Architecture* (translation of the 1928 printing of *Vers une Architecture*), Frances Lincoln Ltd, London, 2007

Lichtenstein, Claude and Thomas Schregenberger (eds), *As Found: The Discovery of the Ordinary*, Lars Müller Publishers, Baden, 2001

McCarthy, Fiona, *William Morris: A Life for Our Time*, Faber and Faber, London, 2003

Salter, Peter and others, *Sergison Bates Architects: Brick-Work: Thinking and Making*, GTA Verlag, Zurich, 2005

Smithson, Alison and Peter Smithson, *The Charged Void: Architecture*, Monacelli Press, New York, 2002

Stonehouse, Roger, *Trevor Dannatt: Works and Words*, Black Dog Publishing, London, 2008

Ursprung, Philip, *Caruso St John*, Ediciones Polígrafa, Barcelona, 2009

Venturi, Robert, *Complexity and Contradiction in Architecture*, Doubleday, Garden City, New York, 1966

Vitruvius, *On Architecture*, Penguin, London, 2009

Wilson, Colin St John, *Architectural Reflections: Studies in the Philosophy and Practice of Architecture*, Architectural Press, London, 1992

Zumthor, Peter, *Thinking Architecture*, Birkhauser, Basel, 2006

INDEX

PICTURE CREDITS

ACKNOWLEDGEMENTS

The authors would like to thank all the architects, designers and photographers who contributed projects, images and information for this book. We are especially grateful to the designers, Sarah Douglas and Lee Belcher, as well as to Anna Stathaki for her extensive picture research and photography. Many thanks to John Jervis and Philip Cooper at Laurence King for their support of the project.

Jonathan Bell would like to thank Alex, Toby and Pippa. Ellie Stathaki would like to thank her parents and Dimitris.